Satyam Tripathi

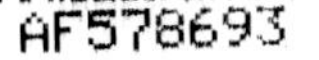

10 INDIAN FAILED STARTUPS

Lessons from Ambition, Innovation, and Market Realities

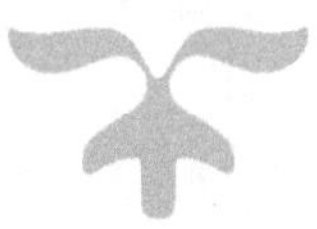

SATYAM TRIPATHI

Copyright Page

10 Indian Failed Startups: Lessons from Ambition, Innovation, and Market Realities

First Edition, 2024

Preface

In the rapidly evolving landscape of Indian startups, countless ventures emerge each year, driven by ambitious visions, innovative ideas, and the hope of transforming industries. However, while the stories of successful unicorns like Flipkart and Zomato dominate the headlines, there is an equally compelling side of the narrative—the stories of failure. These stories, often overshadowed by the glitz of success, carry invaluable lessons about ambition, market realities, and the harsh truths that come with building a business in a competitive environment.

"10 Indian Failed Startups: Lessons from Ambition, Innovation, and Market Realities" delves deep into the journeys of ten startups that began with great promise but ultimately succumbed to the challenges of scaling, differentiation, market misalignment, and financial mismanagement. These are not stories of incompetence or lack of vision. Rather, they are tales of startups that dared to challenge the status quo, only to be met with the harsh realities of execution, competition, and sustainability.

In this book, we explore the rise and fall of ten notable Indian startups—**Stayzilla, PepperTap, TinyOwl, FranklyMe, AskMe, Dazo, iTiffin, Fynd, Yebhi,** and **Zeppery**. Each chapter highlights a different set of challenges that these ventures faced, from scaling issues and logistical failures to cash burn, customer churn, and the inability to secure adequate funding. These stories are not just about failure; they are about the lessons learned from the struggles, the pivots that came too late, and the market realities that even the most innovative ideas couldn't overcome.

For entrepreneurs, investors, and aspiring business leaders, this book offers a candid look at the intricacies of the startup ecosystem. It sheds light on the importance of strategic foresight, operational efficiency, financial discipline, and the need for adaptability in a constantly changing market. As much as these stories highlight the pitfalls of startup culture, they also provide a rich source of insights that can guide future ventures toward sustainable growth and success.

Through these pages, we hope to encourage thoughtful reflection on what it takes to succeed in the world of startups and, more importantly, what it takes to avoid failure. Each of these stories, while ending in closure, is a testament to the resilience, innovation, and relentless pursuit of dreams that characterize the startup ecosystem. In learning from their mistakes, we move one step closer to building the successful startups of tomorrow.

Sincerely,
Satyam Tripathi

About the Author

Satyam Tripathi is an aspiring lawyer, dynamic public speaker, and young entrepreneur with a fervent passion for business. From an early age, Satyam has been drawn to the world of entrepreneurship, driven by a desire to create and inspire. His journey into business has provided him with firsthand experience of the highs and lows of building something from scratch, allowing him to gain invaluable insights into what it takes to succeed in today's competitive landscape.

In addition to his entrepreneurial pursuits, Satyam is a dedicated mentor to young people, committed to guiding the next generation of leaders. He strongly believes that with the right mindset and tools, anyone can turn their dreams into reality. Through his speeches and writings, he offers practical advice on overcoming obstacles, navigating uncertainties, and taking bold steps toward success. His goal is to demystify the startup process and empower individuals to take control of their futures.

Satyam's mission is not only to build successful businesses but to inspire and equip others to do the same. He views entrepreneurship as a powerful tool for personal growth and societal impact and is dedicated to helping young dreamers transform their ideas into thriving ventures.

Contents

Chapter 1. Stayzilla: Scaling Ambition, Missteps, and the Fall of India's Pioneer in Budget Stays

1. Introduction to Stayzilla

Stayzilla was founded in 2005 by three enterprising individuals: Yogendra Vasupal, Sachit Singhi, and Hemanth Rao. Originally named Inasra.com, the platform rebranded to Stayzilla in 2010, setting its sights on becoming a leader in the budget hotel aggregation market in India. The founders, driven by a vision to make travel accommodations more accessible, aimed to offer travelers affordable hotel stays across both urban and rural areas. Their goal was to connect people with a wide range of budget accommodations that were previously hard to access.

Stayzilla's founders recognized the untapped potential in India's rapidly expanding travel and tourism industry, especially the highly fragmented budget hotel sector. With domestic travel growing, especially in Tier 2 and Tier 3 cities, there was a significant gap between demand for budget hotels and the supply of organized, bookable stays. Stayzilla aimed to fill this gap by offering a seamless platform that brought together affordable lodging options, even in remote locations.

The platform differentiated itself by not only focusing on urban centers but also expanding into rural and lesser-known destinations. This unique positioning allowed Stayzilla to cater to a broader audience, from business travelers to backpackers, who sought affordable accommodation across India. By creating a comprehensive network of hotels in regions often overlooked by competitors, Stayzilla sought to build a niche for itself and become a key player in the travel industry.

Stayzilla's vision and early success captured the attention of both investors and consumers. The founders' ambition to bridge the gap between affordable stays and travelers' needs made them pioneers in the Indian travel ecosystem. However, as Stayzilla grew, it faced increasing challenges that eventually led to its decline, but its initial vision of democratizing travel accommodations remains an important part of its legacy.

2. The Idea and Initial Success

Stayzilla's idea was simple but impactful: to create a platform that would make budget hotels easily accessible, especially in lesser-known towns across India. The founders understood that many travelers, particularly in Tier 2 and Tier 3 cities, struggled to find affordable and reliable lodging. This early focus on small-town accommodations set Stayzilla apart from its competitors, who were more concentrated on metropolitan areas. The platform quickly gained traction as it tapped into an untapped market, helping budget-conscious travelers discover new destinations without breaking the bank.

The company's innovative approach and focus on previously ignored areas caught the attention of investors. In its growth phase, Stayzilla raised $33 million in venture funding from investors, including Nexus Venture Partners and Matrix Partners India. This funding allowed Stayzilla to expand its services and improve its platform, giving the company the resources it needed to scale. The funding milestone signified the faith that investors had in the platform's potential to revolutionize the budget hotel market in India.

With this backing, Stayzilla began focusing on a larger expansion plan, aiming to establish a stronghold in Tier 2 and Tier 3 cities. These cities represented a growing segment of travelers who were increasingly looking for budget travel options. The company's strategy was to build a network of small hotels in areas where competitors had little or no presence, making Stayzilla the go-to platform for those seeking budget accommodations in emerging travel destinations.

Stayzilla's early success was driven by its clear vision and ability to meet the needs of a diverse and growing market. By expanding its services to rural and small-town areas, Stayzilla was able to provide affordable options to millions of travelers. The platform's initial momentum established Stayzilla as a pioneer in budget accommodations, but as the company continued to grow, it would soon face challenges that would test its operational and business model.

3. Scaling Issues Begin to Surface

As Stayzilla began to expand aggressively into smaller towns and rural markets, the company faced a number of challenges that made scaling more difficult than anticipated. One of the major hurdles was maintaining strong relationships with the small hoteliers who formed the backbone of their offering. These hoteliers were often not tech-savvy and had little experience in working with large platforms. Convincing them to list their properties on Stayzilla and operate under a uniform pricing and service structure required significant effort. Additionally, these partnerships were prone to friction, especially as some hoteliers expressed concerns over payment delays and inconsistencies in booking volumes.

Operational costs started to mount as Stayzilla tried to penetrate smaller, less accessible markets. While the company had positioned itself as a platform for budget accommodations, the reality of managing properties in remote areas brought higher costs, such as logistics, customer service, and onboarding. Unlike urban areas where infrastructure and support systems were robust, these smaller markets often lacked the basic resources necessary for seamless operations, making it expensive to maintain listings and ensure customer satisfaction. This increased overhead put pressure on Stayzilla's bottom line, despite the growing number of hotels on its platform.

Another significant issue was the difficulty in maintaining a standardized customer experience across diverse regions. As Stayzilla expanded its reach, it became increasingly challenging to enforce consistent service levels and quality control. The platform catered to a wide range of accommodations, from budget hotels in metropolitan cities to small guesthouses in rural areas. Ensuring that these varied properties adhered to uniform standards—such as cleanliness, customer service, and amenities—became a logistical nightmare. Customers often complained about discrepancies in the quality of stay, leading to dissatisfaction and negative reviews that began to hurt the brand's reputation.

These operational challenges were exacerbated by Stayzilla's rapid growth, which placed even more strain on the company's resources. The company had expanded too quickly, without fully considering the complexities of managing such a widespread network of hotels. As Stayzilla scaled, the company found itself juggling too many priorities—managing vendor relationships, dealing with high operational costs, and ensuring a good customer experience. This lack of focus contributed to mounting inefficiencies and weakened the company's ability to sustain its growth trajectory.

Ultimately, Stayzilla's ambitious expansion plan, while well-intentioned, led to significant scaling issues that the company was ill-prepared to handle. The cost of managing a large, dispersed network of properties, combined with the inability to ensure a consistent customer experience, would later contribute to the company's downfall. These challenges underscored the importance of a sustainable, well-thought-out growth strategy—something that Stayzilla struggled to implement as it grew.

4. Competition and Market Misalignment

As Stayzilla continued to expand, it faced intense competition, particularly from OYO Rooms, which was aggressively capturing the urban budget hotel market. Unlike Stayzilla, which had focused on rural and Tier 2/3 cities, OYO took a more concentrated approach, targeting large urban centers where demand for budget accommodation was more consistent and profitable. OYO's strategy was to establish a strong foothold in metropolitan cities, offering a more standardized and tech-driven experience, which appealed to a broader customer base, including business travelers and tourists looking for affordable but reliable options.

The contrast in approaches between Stayzilla and OYO became evident as OYO's dominance in urban markets began to grow. OYO's model prioritized consistent quality, transparency, and a seamless booking process through its app, giving it a competitive edge. Meanwhile, Stayzilla's focus on rural and budget markets, while innovative, proved to be a double-edged sword. While there was demand in these smaller markets, the unpredictable nature of these regions made it harder for Stayzilla to build the same level of brand loyalty and customer trust that OYO was able to generate in cities. This allowed OYO to quickly outpace Stayzilla in terms of market share and visibility.

A significant challenge for Stayzilla was the misalignment between its offerings and customer expectations. While the company initially sought to capture the rural market, many customers who used the platform were travelers expecting a certain level of service and consistency, which Stayzilla struggled to provide in less developed areas. Unlike OYO, which streamlined its offerings to ensure a standardized experience regardless of location, Stayzilla's focus on budget accommodations in disparate regions resulted in wide variations in service quality. This left many customers disappointed, as their experiences didn't match their expectations, leading to negative reviews and loss of repeat business.

The difference in strategy also exposed Stayzilla's vulnerability to changing market dynamics. OYO, by focusing on urban markets and business travelers, was able to quickly attract investment and expand its offerings, including providing additional services like on-site assistance and guaranteed amenities. Stayzilla, on the other hand, remained entrenched in rural markets that were harder to scale, limiting its ability to diversify and pivot as the market evolved. This divergence in focus placed Stayzilla at a disadvantage, especially as consumer preferences increasingly shifted towards convenience and standardization.

In the end, Stayzilla's misaligned market strategy became one of its biggest weaknesses. By focusing on rural and budget accommodations while its competitors like OYO dominated urban markets with more scalable models, Stayzilla struggled to keep up. The misfit between what the platform offered and what customers wanted further deepened Stayzilla's challenges, highlighting the importance of aligning market strategy with customer expectations in a rapidly evolving industry.

5. Fundraising and Rapid Expansion

Stayzilla's journey saw a significant boost when it successfully raised $33 million in venture funding, with investors like Nexus Venture Partners backing the company. This influx of capital was meant to fuel the startup's ambitious growth plans, particularly its efforts to capture the under-served rural and Tier 2/3 markets. The funding gave Stayzilla the resources to aggressively expand its operations, onboard more hotels, and establish itself as a key player in India's burgeoning travel and hospitality sector. The idea was to build a robust network of budget accommodations across regions often overlooked by other competitors.

However, the decision to expand rapidly into rural areas came with its own set of challenges. While the rural market was less saturated, it was also far more difficult to manage operationally. Expanding into these areas required considerable resources in terms of infrastructure, marketing, and operational support, far beyond what Stayzilla had anticipated. The company's leadership believed that by being the first-mover in these markets, they would gain a competitive advantage. However, the reality proved different, as maintaining the quality of service and consistency across these dispersed regions became increasingly challenging.

Despite its aggressive expansion strategy, Stayzilla faced a major roadblock when it came to profitability. While the company did manage to grow in terms of the number of hotels listed on its platform, this growth did not translate into sustainable profits. The cost of acquiring new properties and managing operations in rural and remote areas far outweighed the revenue generated from these listings. Additionally, customer acquisition costs were high, and the unpredictable nature of demand in smaller towns made it difficult to achieve the economies of scale needed to break even. This created a significant cash burn, putting immense pressure on the company to either scale faster or change its approach.

In the end, Stayzilla's rapid expansion stretched its resources too thin, both financially and operationally. The focus on growth at all costs led to a situation where the company's expenses far outpaced its revenues. While Stayzilla managed to build an extensive network of hotels, it was unable to sustain this expansion profitably. The challenges of maintaining service quality, meeting customer expectations, and managing vendor relationships in these remote areas proved to be too much, marking the beginning of the company's decline.

6. Challenges with Vendor Relations

One of the significant challenges Stayzilla faced during its expansion was the difficulty in maintaining consistent relations with hoteliers, especially in rural areas. Unlike urban regions, where professional hospitality services were more streamlined, rural hoteliers often operated on informal agreements. This made it challenging for Stayzilla to establish and sustain reliable partnerships. The company found it hard to standardize expectations and ensure that all hoteliers provided the same quality of service to customers, leading to inconsistencies in the user experience.

Additionally, many hoteliers began to complain about delayed payments from Stayzilla. With an increasing number of properties being added to the platform, Stayzilla struggled to manage cash flow efficiently. Operational inefficiencies, coupled with a strained financial model, led to significant delays in compensating the hoteliers. These delays not only affected Stayzilla's reputation but also created frustration among the hotel owners, some of whom depended on timely payments to run their operations smoothly. The financial strain became an ongoing issue, leading to dissatisfaction from the vendor side.

This financial and operational disconnect led to growing trust issues with smaller hoteliers, particularly in rural markets, where relationships were built more on personal trust than formal contracts. As a result, many hotel owners began to distance themselves from Stayzilla, feeling that the platform was unreliable and unable to deliver on its promises. This damaged Stayzilla's brand, making it harder to build new partnerships and retain existing ones, especially as competitors like OYO gained traction with more reliable models.

7. Operational and Management Struggles

As Stayzilla continued to expand, the company began to face significant operational inefficiencies in managing its growing portfolio of listings, customer bookings, and payments. The complexity of handling hundreds of hotel partners across diverse regions—each with its own set of challenges—proved overwhelming. Managing customer bookings became a logistical nightmare, as inconsistencies in hotel quality and availability led to frequent customer complaints. Payments to hoteliers were often delayed due to Stayzilla's cash flow issues, further complicating vendor relationships. This operational mismanagement caused the overall service quality to decline, eroding customer trust.

Another major issue was the leadership's struggle to scale the business effectively. While the founders had a clear vision, the lack of experienced personnel with expertise in managing large-scale operations became evident. The company expanded too quickly without a solid operational backbone, leaving it vulnerable to internal mismanagement. The absence of a structured leadership team capable of guiding the company through its rapid growth phase meant that key decisions were often delayed or poorly executed, leading to further inefficiencies in day-to-day operations.

The company also faced a high employee turnover rate as Stayzilla's internal challenges mounted. Employees became disillusioned with the constant operational problems and lack of a clear direction from leadership. This turnover resulted in a loss of institutional knowledge and further disrupted operations, as the company constantly had to recruit and train new employees. In a fast-paced environment, this lack of stability at the employee level created additional strain on the already overburdened systems. With these issues piling up, management was unable to implement effective solutions in time to save the company. Stayzilla's leadership found itself caught between the need to scale and the inability to manage its current operations efficiently. The company's failure to build a sustainable and well-organized operational infrastructure ultimately led to its downfall, as the problems with vendors, employees, and customers spiraled out of control.

8. The Decline of Stayzilla

In February 2017, Stayzilla made a shocking announcement that it would be halting operations, marking the end of a once-promising startup in India's hospitality sector. Despite its early success and significant funding, Stayzilla was unable to sustain its growth. The company's journey, which had started with grand ambitions to connect rural and urban travelers with budget accommodations, came to an abrupt halt due to mounting challenges that it could no longer manage. This announcement sent shockwaves through the Indian startup ecosystem, as Stayzilla had been viewed as a pioneer in the hospitality-tech space.

One of the primary reasons for Stayzilla's shutdown was its inability to scale profitably. While the company expanded aggressively into rural markets and listed thousands of budget accommodations, it struggled to turn this growth into profit. The business model, heavily reliant on rural and small-town markets, was inherently challenging. The operational costs associated with servicing these areas were high, and the revenue generated was not enough to cover these expenses. This imbalance resulted in a severe cash burn that the company was unable to recover from, despite multiple rounds of venture capital funding.

Stayzilla also suffered from a misaligned market strategy. While its focus on rural areas and smaller markets differentiated it from competitors, it also limited its ability to compete with players like OYO, which concentrated on urban centers with higher demand and profitability. Stayzilla's strategy of doing too many things—trying to be a comprehensive aggregator across diverse markets—spread its resources too thin. The company couldn't maintain the quality or consistency needed to meet customer expectations, leading to dissatisfaction and a gradual loss of market share to competitors.

In his farewell note, Stayzilla's founder, Yogendra Vasupal, famously remarked that they had been "trying to do too many things", which ultimately led to the company's downfall. The desire to capture both rural and urban markets, while catering to budget travelers, left Stayzilla overstretched and unable to focus on what could have been its core strengths. The startup's journey ended as a cautionary tale about the dangers of scaling too quickly without a clear, sustainable path to profitability, leaving valuable lessons for future entrepreneurs.

9. Legal Battles and Controversies

After Stayzilla ceased operations, the company and its founder, Yogendra Vasupal, found themselves embroiled in a legal storm. In a dramatic turn of events, Vasupal was arrested on charges of unpaid dues, which were filed by an advertising agency that claimed Stayzilla owed them money for services rendered. The arrest shocked many in India's startup community, as it highlighted the severe consequences that founders can face when a business fails. Vasupal's case quickly became a lightning rod for broader discussions on the risks and responsibilities of entrepreneurship in India.

The legal battle raised significant concerns about the treatment of entrepreneurs in the country. Many argued that Vasupal's arrest was unjust, as it set a dangerous precedent for how failed startups and founders could be criminalized for business disputes. This sparked a debate about the need for better protections and support systems for entrepreneurs, who often take on substantial personal and financial risks in their ventures. Vasupal himself voiced these concerns, stating that the pressure on founders can be overwhelming, especially when the legal system becomes involved in what is, at its core, a commercial failure.

The industry response to Stayzilla's legal troubles was sharply divided. On one hand, many within the startup ecosystem rallied around Vasupal, viewing him as a victim of an unfair system that penalized risk-taking. Several prominent entrepreneurs and venture capitalists voiced their support, advocating for the need to create an environment where founders could fail without fear of personal legal consequences. On the other hand, some critics pointed to mismanagement and poor financial discipline as the root causes of Stayzilla's downfall, suggesting that the company's leadership failed to maintain adequate business practices that could have prevented such disputes.

This controversy also highlighted the fragility of the Indian startup ecosystem. For many, Vasupal's arrest symbolized the larger issue of how easily startups can be derailed by financial and legal complications. The situation drew attention to the fact that while India had become a hotbed for innovation and entrepreneurial activity, its infrastructure for supporting businesses—especially when they faced difficulties—was still lacking. This led to calls for reforms, particularly around bankruptcy laws and the legal rights of founders.

Ultimately, the Stayzilla saga became a cautionary tale not just about the challenges of scaling a business, but also about the risks involved in navigating India's complex legal and financial landscape as an entrepreneur. It underscored the importance of balancing ambition with operational discipline and the need for greater institutional support for startups facing crises.

10. Industry Impact and Competitors

Stayzilla's collapse sent ripples through the Indian startup ecosystem, raising critical questions about the feasibility of scaling businesses in India's hospitality sector, especially in rural and budget markets. It became evident that scaling too quickly without strong operational infrastructure could lead to catastrophic failures. Stayzilla's ambitious goal of catering to both urban and rural customers proved difficult to manage, prompting a broader reflection within the industry about the challenges of expanding in a highly fragmented and diverse market like India.

The fall of Stayzilla coincided with the meteoric rise of OYO Rooms, which quickly filled the gap left behind. Unlike Stayzilla, OYO shifted its focus to the urban budget hotel sector, aggressively expanding its network in Tier 1 and Tier 2 cities. By streamlining its business model and focusing on standardizing customer experiences, OYO was able to capture a large portion of the market. OYO's strategy of partnering with existing hotels and ensuring a standardized experience for customers, even in budget accommodations, became a cornerstone of its success. This strategic shift allowed OYO to avoid the pitfalls that Stayzilla encountered with inconsistent rural listings and operational inefficiencies.

The contrast between OYO's success and Stayzilla's failure served as a valuable lesson for other startups in the Indian ecosystem. Startups realized the importance of focusing on one core market segment rather than trying to cater to too many different demographics at once. Stayzilla's downfall taught founders that while rural markets in India present a massive opportunity, they also come with unique challenges, such as infrastructure limitations and difficulty in maintaining relationships with small vendors. This case demonstrated that scaling in India requires a more thoughtful and incremental approach, particularly in sectors like hospitality that rely heavily on vendor partnerships.

Additionally, Stayzilla's story highlighted the need for sustainable growth over aggressive expansion. The pressure to grow quickly, fueled by venture capital funding, can lead to unsustainable practices, such as poor cash flow management and unchecked operational costs. Startups learned that raising capital is only one part of the puzzle; building a robust operational backbone is equally essential for long-term success.

Overall, Stayzilla's demise became a cautionary tale in India's entrepreneurial landscape, emphasizing the importance of strategic planning, market alignment, and operational excellence. The lessons from Stayzilla's failure helped shape the approach of newer startups, pushing them to be more mindful of the challenges that come with scaling, especially in sectors that require extensive logistical coordination and vendor management.

11. Lessons Learned from Stayzilla

The story of Stayzilla offers several critical lessons for entrepreneurs, particularly in the realm of cash flow management during rapid scaling. One of the most significant factors contributing to Stayzilla's downfall was its inability to maintain a healthy cash flow amid aggressive expansion efforts. Startups often face immense pressure to grow quickly and attract investors, which can lead to overlooking fundamental financial principles. Entrepreneurs must prioritize maintaining liquidity to navigate operational challenges and unforeseen expenses, ensuring they have enough runway to execute their strategies without compromising on service quality.

Another key takeaway is the need for a customer-centric approach rather than purely business-driven decisions. Stayzilla initially found success by addressing a niche market of budget travelers in lesser-known towns, but as it scaled, the focus shifted away from the needs and expectations of its customers. Startups should ensure that their strategies align with customer desires and preferences, as neglecting customer experience can lead to brand loyalty erosion. In a competitive landscape, understanding customer pain points and delivering solutions that resonate with them is paramount for sustainable success.

The importance of having a strong operational backbone to support large-scale expansion cannot be overstated. Stayzilla's operational challenges, such as managing relationships with small hoteliers and ensuring a consistent guest experience, hindered its ability to scale effectively. For startups aiming to grow, it's crucial to establish efficient processes and robust systems from the outset. This foundation allows for seamless operations, which in turn fosters positive customer experiences and can significantly reduce operational inefficiencies as the business scales.

Furthermore, balancing growth and stability is essential. While raising funds and expanding aggressively might seem appealing, startups must also ensure they are building a sustainable business model. Learning from Stayzilla, new entrepreneurs should focus on creating a scalable model that does not compromise quality for growth. A well-thought-out strategy that balances expansion with operational stability is crucial for long-term success in the competitive startup landscape.

Lastly, the narrative of Stayzilla serves as a reminder that adaptability is key in the ever-evolving startup ecosystem. The ability to pivot in response to market demands, competition, and internal challenges can be the difference between success and failure. Startups should be prepared to reassess their strategies and make necessary adjustments as they grow, ensuring they remain aligned with both their mission and the needs of their target audience. Embracing a culture of adaptability will empower entrepreneurs to navigate challenges more effectively and leverage opportunities that arise in their journey.

12. What Happened to the Founders

After the closure of Stayzilla, Yogendra Vasupal, the co-founder, embarked on a new journey advocating for founder rights and raising awareness about the challenges entrepreneurs face in the startup ecosystem. He became a vocal advocate for the treatment of entrepreneurs in India, highlighting the need for better support systems and protections for founders facing financial and legal challenges. His experiences with Stayzilla inspired him to engage with various startup communities and organizations, where he shared his insights and experiences to help other entrepreneurs avoid similar pitfalls.

While Vasupal took on a public role, the other co-founders, Sachit Singhi and Hemanth Rao, also remained active in the startup ecosystem. They explored new ventures, leveraging their experiences from Stayzilla to contribute to various initiatives. Their knowledge of the hospitality and technology sectors positioned them to offer valuable insights and mentorship to emerging entrepreneurs. Through networking and collaborating with others, they continued to play a part in shaping the Indian startup landscape, contributing to new projects and startups that align with their vision.

As they reflected on their startup journey, the founders acknowledged the lessons learned from their experience with Stayzilla. They discussed the importance of resilience, adaptability, and maintaining a customer-centric approach. Each founder recognized that their journey was not just about success or failure; it was about growth and learning through every challenge they faced. They often shared stories of the highs and lows they experienced, emphasizing that the entrepreneurial path is fraught with uncertainties that can lead to valuable insights.

Moreover, the experience of running Stayzilla served as a catalyst for the founders to focus on community building within the startup ecosystem. They became involved in mentorship programs, startup incubators, and workshops aimed at supporting budding entrepreneurs. By sharing their experiences and offering guidance, they aimed to help the next generation of founders navigate the complexities of building and scaling a startup, ultimately fostering a more robust and supportive ecosystem.

In conclusion, the post-Stayzilla journey for the founders encapsulated a blend of advocacy, mentorship, and reflection. Their experiences, both challenging and rewarding, equipped them with the tools to contribute positively to the entrepreneurial community. By emphasizing the need for a supportive environment for founders, they not only sought to uplift their own narratives but also inspired others to embrace the entrepreneurial spirit while being mindful of the lessons learned from the past.

Key Points

- **Stayzilla's journey** highlights the challenges Indian startups face in scaling within a competitive environment, emphasizing the need for strategic planning and adaptability in the rapidly evolving budget accommodation sector.
- **The company's downfall** demonstrates the importance of aligning ambitious growth plans with operational capabilities to avoid resource strain, inefficiencies, and service breakdowns.

- **Stayzilla's impact** on India's budget accommodation sector was significant, but its failure underscores the need for robust operational frameworks and strong vendor relationships to ensure sustainable growth.
- **Operational inefficiencies and vendor dissatisfaction** were critical factors in Stayzilla's decline, as the company struggled to maintain consistency while scaling across different regions.
- **Stayzilla's story** offers a valuable lesson for future entrepreneurs on the importance of strategic execution, adaptability, and learning from failures to build resilient and sustainable businesses.

Chapter 2. PepperTap: The Rise and Fall of a Hyperlocal Dream

1. Introduction to PepperTap

PepperTap emerged in 2014 as an on-demand grocery delivery platform, catering to the growing demand for hyperlocal delivery services in India's fast-evolving e-commerce landscape. Founded by Navneet Singh and Milind Sharma, the platform was positioned to capitalize on the convenience-driven urban population that was increasingly leaning towards online shopping. PepperTap sought to provide a solution for time-strapped consumers by offering quick and efficient grocery deliveries, a concept that was gaining popularity in many metropolitan cities across the country.

The startup gained traction quickly, particularly in cities like Delhi, Mumbai, and Bangalore, where consumers appreciated the convenience of having groceries delivered to their doorsteps within a matter of hours. The platform was lauded for its speed and ease of use, allowing users to order everyday essentials through a simple mobile app. This fast adoption in urban areas signaled that PepperTap had tapped into a significant market opportunity, promising to disrupt the traditional grocery shopping experience.

PepperTap's business model was built on the hyperlocal delivery framework, wherein it partnered with local grocery stores to fulfill customer orders. This model allowed the company to keep its inventory costs low while providing a broad range of products to consumers. The idea of leveraging existing grocery stores rather than establishing its warehouses gave PepperTap the flexibility to scale rapidly. By bridging the gap between consumers and local vendors, PepperTap created a win-win situation for both parties, as vendors gained access to new customers and increased sales while consumers enjoyed the convenience of home delivery.

The timing of PepperTap's launch coincided with India's rising interest in e-commerce, spurred by the increasing penetration of smartphones and affordable internet. The hyperlocal delivery model was seen as the next frontier in online retail, with the promise of quick delivery in densely populated urban areas. In the context of India's fast-paced urbanization and the growing middle class, platforms like PepperTap were poised for rapid growth, with many seeing it as the future of grocery shopping in the country.

PepperTap's rise also reflected the broader shift in consumer behavior in India, where convenience was becoming a critical factor in purchasing decisions. As people moved away from traditional brick-and-mortar shopping, the demand for online delivery services increased. PepperTap was one of several startups vying for a share in this emerging market, alongside competitors like Grofers and BigBasket. Each was focused on capturing a slice of the fast-growing grocery delivery sector, a market that had massive potential given India's burgeoning urban population.

The founders, Navneet Singh and Milind Sharma, were seasoned entrepreneurs who identified the gaps in the grocery shopping experience. They realized that for many urban consumers, time was a premium, and grocery shopping was a time-consuming task that could be streamlined with technology. With this insight, they built a platform that catered to the modern consumer, delivering groceries at the click of a button. The startup's early success indicated that they had struck the right chord with their target audience, positioning PepperTap as a promising player in the hyperlocal delivery space.

In its initial stages, PepperTap also benefitted from the growing investor interest in hyperlocal delivery startups. Venture capitalists saw potential in PepperTap's business model, which addressed the logistical challenges of last-mile delivery in urban areas. The company's focus on speed and convenience resonated with both consumers and investors alike, as it seemed to be the perfect solution to the evolving demands of India's urban population.

However, as PepperTap expanded and scaled its operations across multiple cities, it became clear that managing the complexities of hyperlocal delivery would not be as straightforward as initially envisioned. The company's rapid growth came with its own set of challenges, from logistical issues to operational inefficiencies, which would ultimately shape the trajectory of its journey in the highly competitive e-commerce space.

2. Early Success

PepperTap quickly positioned itself as one of the leading players in India's emerging on-demand grocery delivery space. The startup was launched at a time when convenience became a key selling point for urban consumers, and PepperTap capitalized on this demand with its promise of rapid delivery. The platform allowed users to browse, order, and receive groceries from local vendors in a matter of hours, catering to the fast-paced lifestyle of urbanites who valued time over the traditional shopping experience. This convenience factor helped PepperTap gain significant traction among its target audience almost immediately.

In its first year of operation, PepperTap saw impressive user base growth, reflecting the company's success in meeting the needs of its customers. The seamless app experience played a crucial role in this growth. The app's intuitive design and ease of use allowed consumers to quickly place orders from the comfort of their homes, eliminating the hassle of visiting crowded grocery stores. The platform's ability to provide a wide range of products from multiple local vendors made it a one-stop solution for grocery shopping, further enhancing its appeal.

One of the major factors behind PepperTap's early success was its strategic partnerships with local grocers. Instead of managing its own inventory, PepperTap collaborated with small neighborhood stores to fulfill customer orders. This approach not only allowed the company to offer a diverse product range without the need for warehousing but also helped local grocers expand their customer base by reaching consumers who preferred online shopping. This win-win situation enabled PepperTap to scale quickly while maintaining low operational costs, a key advantage in the hyperlocal delivery sector.

To fuel its expansion, PepperTap raised an impressive $40 million in funding from investors such as Sequoia Capital, SAIF Partners, and others. This influx of capital allowed the company to expand its operations across multiple cities in India, including major metropolitan areas like Delhi, Mumbai, and Bengaluru. The funding was used to bolster the company's infrastructure, enhance its technology, and expand its delivery network, positioning PepperTap for rapid growth. The strong backing from investors highlighted the immense potential of the on-demand grocery delivery model, which was becoming an integral part of India's e-commerce landscape.

The timing of PepperTap's launch also worked in its favor. With the growing penetration of smartphones and affordable mobile data, more people were turning to mobile apps for their daily needs. PepperTap's mobile-first strategy tapped into this trend, making it easy for customers to order groceries on the go. This focus on mobile convenience, combined with its partnerships with local vendors, allowed PepperTap to scale at a remarkable pace during its initial phase of growth. The company quickly became a household name in India's urban centers, recognized for its reliability and speed of service.

Despite the early success, PepperTap's rapid expansion would soon present challenges, particularly in managing its logistical operations at scale. However, in its first year, the company demonstrated a keen understanding of consumer preferences and leveraged them to create a strong foundation for growth. Its early success in achieving a large user base and attracting significant venture funding set the stage for its aggressive push to dominate the hyperlocal delivery market.

3. Rapid Expansion Plans

PepperTap's early success and growing consumer base led to ambitious expansion plans as the company sought to scale aggressively across India. After establishing a strong foothold in major Tier 1 cities like Delhi, Mumbai, and Bengaluru, PepperTap set its sights on penetrating Tier 2 cities as well. The goal was to bring the convenience of on-demand grocery delivery to a wider audience, tapping into the untapped potential of smaller urban centers where the e-commerce wave was starting to gain momentum. This aggressive expansion strategy was driven by the belief that hyperlocal delivery services could thrive in regions with growing consumer demand for convenience.

With competitors like BigBasket and Grofers already making headway in the grocery delivery space, PepperTap recognized the need to act quickly to gain a competitive edge. To compete with these established players, PepperTap aimed to offer a superior user experience, faster delivery times, and a more diverse selection of products sourced from local grocers. The company also planned to leverage its existing partnerships with vendors to support its growing customer base. PepperTap's strategy was to outpace its competitors by rapidly increasing its presence across India and becoming the go-to platform for grocery deliveries.

In 2015, PepperTap set an ambitious goal of expanding its operations to 35 cities within the year. This decision reflected the company's determination to dominate the grocery delivery market by reaching more customers and scaling its operations quickly. However, while the expansion plan was bold, it also came with significant challenges in logistics, infrastructure, and management, which would soon become critical factors in the company's journey.

4. Funding and Scaling Up

PepperTap's aggressive expansion plans were backed by significant financial support from prominent investors. The company secured additional funding from Sequoia Capital and SAIF Partners, raising over $40 million in total. This infusion of capital gave PepperTap the resources needed to fuel its growth ambitions and scale up its operations across India. With this funding, the company was able to expand its delivery network, partner with more local grocers, and enhance its mobile app to improve the customer experience. The rapid injection of capital also helped PepperTap establish a strong presence in multiple cities, marking its entry into new urban markets.

The expansion allowed PepperTap to reach a wider audience, especially in cities where the demand for hyperlocal delivery was still emerging. With the financial backing from leading venture capital firms, the company had the flexibility to explore new markets, invest in marketing, and build its operational infrastructure. However, scaling up such an operationally intense business also brought significant challenges. Managing a large network of local vendors, ensuring timely deliveries, and maintaining customer satisfaction across different regions became increasingly difficult as the business grew.

One of the major hurdles PepperTap faced was the logistical complexity of grocery delivery. Unlike other e-commerce platforms, grocery deliveries require precise inventory management, real-time coordination with vendors, and efficient last-mile delivery solutions. As the company expanded into more cities, the costs associated with managing deliveries, handling perishable goods, and maintaining a seamless customer experience began to rise rapidly. This operational intensity placed enormous pressure on the company's ability to execute efficiently at scale.

While the funding allowed PepperTap to grow quickly, the company's operational backbone struggled to keep pace with its expansion. As the challenges of scaling became more apparent, it became clear that maintaining profitability and ensuring consistent service across cities would require more than just capital—it needed a well-optimized logistical infrastructure, which PepperTap found increasingly hard to achieve.

5. Operational Challenges

As PepperTap expanded its operations across India, the logistical complexities of managing a hyperlocal supply chain began to surface. Unlike traditional e-commerce businesses, PepperTap had to deal with the nuances of grocery delivery, which involved coordinating real-time orders with local grocers, managing inventory of perishable items, and ensuring timely deliveries within short windows. This operational model required seamless execution, and as the business grew, these complexities became increasingly difficult to manage.

One of the biggest challenges was coordinating with multiple local grocers in different cities. PepperTap partnered with a wide range of vendors, each with its own inventory system, pricing, and logistical capabilities. Ensuring that orders were fulfilled accurately and delivered on time was a monumental task, especially as the company expanded to new markets. Inconsistent inventory levels, coupled with communication gaps between the app and local grocers, often led to delayed deliveries or canceled orders, frustrating customers and damaging PepperTap's brand image.

Another key challenge lay in managing the warehousing and supply chain infrastructure. PepperTap initially relied on a "just-in-time" delivery model, which meant they didn't hold inventory but sourced it from local grocers once an order was placed. While this minimized holding costs, it also created significant inefficiencies, as grocers couldn't always fulfill the required quantities on time. Without a centralized inventory system, PepperTap had little control over the stock levels, leading to frequent out-of-stock situations and order cancellations.

The delivery process, which was critical to the customer experience, also faced significant hurdles. As the company expanded to more cities, managing a large fleet of delivery personnel became a challenge. Ensuring timely deliveries in congested urban areas while dealing with unpredictable traffic, weather conditions, and workforce shortages added further complexity. The high cost of maintaining a reliable delivery workforce and the inefficiencies in route optimization led to rising operational costs, which became unsustainable in the long run.

The inefficiencies extended to the backend operations as well. The company struggled to manage its warehouses efficiently, leading to delays in dispatching orders to delivery staff. As the business grew, it became increasingly clear that PepperTap's operational infrastructure was not equipped to handle the volume of orders it was receiving. This mismatch between demand and operational capability led to frequent breakdowns in the supply chain, negatively affecting customer satisfaction and repeat business.

Moreover, the reliance on third-party delivery services and local grocers meant that PepperTap had limited control over the quality of service. If a local vendor failed to fulfill an order or if a delivery was delayed due to external factors, PepperTap bore the brunt of customer dissatisfaction. These issues compounded as the company scaled, highlighting the inherent difficulties of managing a hyperlocal delivery model at such a large scale.

In addition to logistical challenges, PepperTap faced the difficulty of managing a large and dispersed workforce. High employee turnover, particularly among delivery staff, further strained the company's operations. Training new employees and maintaining consistent service standards across cities required a significant investment of time and resources, which became harder to sustain as operational inefficiencies mounted.

6. Competition in the Market

PepperTap's rapid expansion came at a time when the Indian online grocery market was heating up, with major competitors like BigBasket and Grofers vying for market dominance. BigBasket, in particular, had already established itself as a leader in the space, with a well-developed operational model that catered to a wide range of customers. While PepperTap focused on hyperlocal delivery from small grocers, BigBasket had invested heavily in building its own centralized supply chain, ensuring more control over inventory and better customer service.

Grofers, another strong competitor, also followed a hyperlocal model similar to PepperTap, but with a more efficient approach to managing vendors and deliveries. Grofers managed to streamline its operations by integrating technology more effectively, which allowed for better inventory management and smoother communication with local partners. This gave them an edge over PepperTap, which was still struggling to overcome logistical challenges as it scaled its operations. Grofers also provided a more consistent customer experience, which contributed to its growing popularity in the market.

PepperTap's struggle to keep up with its more efficient competitors became increasingly apparent as the market matured. While BigBasket and Grofers were able to maintain higher customer satisfaction by focusing on operational efficiency, PepperTap's reliance on local grocers and third-party delivery services led to inconsistent service quality. Customers often faced delays, out-of-stock items, or incorrect orders, which pushed them toward more reliable alternatives like BigBasket and Grofers.

Ultimately, the competitive pressure from these better-organized companies exposed the weaknesses in PepperTap's business model. The inability to streamline its operations, manage its vendor relationships, and ensure a smooth delivery experience placed the company at a disadvantage in the rapidly growing online grocery market. This competitive landscape, combined with PepperTap's internal struggles, hastened its decline as it failed to keep up with the industry leaders.

7. Customer Experience Issues

As PepperTap expanded its operations across multiple cities, the complexities of managing a hyperlocal supply chain began to impact customer experience significantly. Delivery delays became a common occurrence, primarily due to logistical challenges in coordinating with local grocers and maintaining efficient delivery routes. Customers frequently found themselves waiting longer than expected for their orders, which resulted in growing frustration and dissatisfaction with the service. These delays not only affected immediate sales but also tarnished the brand's reputation as a reliable grocery delivery platform.

The dissatisfaction among customers was further compounded by the inconsistency in service quality. Many users reported issues with the quality of the products delivered, such as expired items or poor-quality fresh produce. These complaints highlighted the challenges PepperTap faced in maintaining strong relationships with local vendors, which directly affected the reliability of their offerings. As word spread about these experiences, potential customers began to question whether they could trust PepperTap for their grocery needs.

In an age where consumer expectations for convenience and reliability are at an all-time high, the consequences of these service failures became increasingly evident. PepperTap's app ratings started to plummet as users took to review platforms to voice their frustrations. A drop in ratings not only discouraged new users from trying the service but also prompted existing customers to seek alternatives. As a result, the company faced a vicious cycle: declining ratings led to reduced customer trust, which in turn resulted in even lower sales.

The culmination of delivery delays, inconsistent product quality, and negative reviews ultimately impacted PepperTap's market position. As the company's customer satisfaction ratings fell, it became increasingly challenging to compete with rivals like BigBasket and Grofers, who prioritized customer experience. This shift in focus from rapid expansion to addressing customer experience issues became a critical factor in determining the long-term viability of PepperTap’s business model.

8. Mismanagement of Resources

As PepperTap attempted to expand rapidly across multiple cities, one of the critical challenges it faced was the mismanagement of resources. The company struggled to effectively utilize its resources in various locations, leading to operational inefficiencies that adversely impacted service delivery. For instance, the staffing levels in certain cities did not align with the demand, resulting in either understaffing or overstaffing, both of which strained the operational budget and diminished overall productivity. This misalignment became particularly evident during peak delivery times, where customers faced longer wait times due to insufficient delivery personnel.

Furthermore, the allocation of warehouse space across cities was often inefficient. Some locations had warehouses that were either too large for their customer base or inadequately stocked, leading to stockouts and delays. In contrast, other areas faced overwhelming backlogs, as the available space was not optimized to handle the volume of goods needed. This lack of strategic planning not only increased operational costs but also hampered the company's ability to fulfill customer orders promptly. The failure to properly manage warehouse logistics hindered PepperTap's goal of becoming a leader in the hyperlocal grocery delivery market.

Financial mismanagement also contributed to the company's struggles. As PepperTap expanded, the need for operational funding grew, yet the financial strategies employed to manage operating costs were often flawed. High overhead costs, combined with the increased expenses associated with maintaining warehouses and hiring delivery personnel, put a strain on the company's finances. The lack of a sustainable financial plan left PepperTap vulnerable to market fluctuations and ultimately reduced its profitability.

In addition, the company's aggressive expansion strategy led to the pursuit of quick growth over sustainable operations. This prioritization meant that resources were often allocated to new market entries without a thorough assessment of each city's viability. As a result, PepperTap found itself with an extensive network of operations that lacked the necessary support and infrastructure to sustain them. This disconnect between ambition and resource management highlighted a significant flaw in the company's strategic approach, which ultimately hindered its performance.

To address these challenges, PepperTap needed to implement more effective resource management strategies. This included conducting comprehensive market analyses before entering new cities, ensuring that warehouse space was optimized for each location's needs, and creating a flexible staffing model that could adapt to varying demand levels. Additionally, prioritizing financial oversight and budgeting could have helped mitigate the negative impacts of rapid expansion on the company's bottom line.

The consequences of resource mismanagement were not limited to operational inefficiencies; they also affected employee morale. Delivery personnel and warehouse staff often faced overwhelming workloads, leading to burnout and higher turnover rates. As employees became frustrated with the lack of support and the pressures of managing increased demand, the company's overall productivity suffered. Maintaining a motivated and adequately supported workforce was crucial for PepperTap's success, and the mismanagement of resources directly undermined this objective.

Ultimately, the mismanagement of resources proved to be a significant factor in PepperTap's decline. The inability to effectively utilize delivery personnel, manage warehouse space efficiently, and maintain sound financial practices created a perfect storm of operational challenges that the company struggled to overcome. As the grocery delivery landscape continued to evolve, it became increasingly clear that sustainable growth required not only ambition but also a solid foundation in resource management and operational efficiency.

In hindsight, the lessons learned from PepperTap's experience serve as a reminder of the critical importance of resource management in the startup ecosystem. For future entrepreneurs, understanding the dynamics of scaling a business while maintaining control over operational costs and resource allocation will be vital in navigating the complexities of the competitive landscape.

9. Cash Burn and Financial Strain

As PepperTap pursued its aggressive expansion strategy, it faced a significant challenge: a high cash burn rate that quickly became unsustainable. The rapid growth aimed at establishing a foothold in various Tier 1 and Tier 2 cities required substantial investment in logistics, personnel, and marketing. This relentless push to scale resulted in the company depleting its financial resources at an alarming rate, leaving little room for error or adaptation. The initial funding of $40 million was quickly drained as operational costs surged, leading to mounting concerns about the company's long-term viability.

Logistics played a crucial role in PepperTap's operational expenses. Managing a hyperlocal delivery network necessitated not only a large workforce of delivery personnel but also significant investments in technology and infrastructure. The cost of fuel, vehicle maintenance, and warehousing added to the financial strain, making it increasingly difficult for the company to maintain profitability. Despite the growing demand for on-demand grocery delivery, the costs associated with scaling operations outweighed the revenue generated, resulting in an unsustainable business model that could not support its rapid ambitions.

In addition to logistical challenges, the financial mismanagement of resources exacerbated the cash burn issue. Poor forecasting and a lack of strategic financial planning meant that PepperTap often found itself caught off guard by rising expenses. Marketing campaigns aimed at increasing brand awareness consumed a large portion of the budget, yet did not yield the anticipated returns on investment. Instead of fostering sustainable growth, these expenditures drained resources that could have been allocated to critical areas such as improving operational efficiencies and enhancing customer experience.

The cumulative effect of these financial strains eventually took a toll on PepperTap's overall health, leading to a loss of investor confidence. As news of the company's cash burn rate and operational difficulties circulated, potential investors grew wary, making it challenging for PepperTap to secure additional funding. This created a vicious cycle: the company needed funds to stabilize operations but was unable to attract investment due to its unsustainable financial practices. In the fiercely competitive grocery delivery market, the inability to manage cash flow effectively ultimately sealed PepperTap's fate, serving as a stark warning to other startups about the critical importance of financial discipline and strategic planning.

10. Leadership Decisions

The leadership decisions made at PepperTap played a pivotal role in shaping the company's trajectory. Initially, the founders' vision was rooted in the ambition to dominate the grocery delivery market by achieving rapid growth. However, this prioritization of speed over operational stability led to critical oversights that would later haunt the organization. The leadership team's relentless focus on expansion often overshadowed the necessity for establishing a solid operational framework, leaving gaps that would ultimately contribute to the company's downfall.

A significant factor in this misalignment was the lack of experienced management within the company. As PepperTap sought to scale its operations, it became apparent that the existing leadership lacked the expertise required to navigate the complexities of managing a large-scale, logistics-intensive business. Many of the key players were first-time entrepreneurs without the prior experience necessary to make informed decisions about operational efficiency, resource allocation, and customer satisfaction. This lack of experience hindered the organization's ability to implement effective systems and processes essential for sustaining growth.

Moreover, a disconnect between the leadership team and the ground realities became increasingly evident. While the founders were focused on the bigger picture and ambitious growth targets, the challenges faced by frontline employees and local managers often went unaddressed. This disconnection led to a gap in communication, preventing critical insights from reaching the leadership team. Consequently, decisions made at the top were often misaligned with the actual operational challenges and customer needs, leading to significant inefficiencies and missed opportunities to adapt to changing market conditions.

Ultimately, the leadership's failure to balance ambition with operational pragmatism contributed to PepperTap's struggle to establish a sustainable business model. The lessons learned from these leadership decisions serve as a reminder for other startups: the importance of having a management team equipped with both vision and operational expertise is crucial for navigating the complexities of scaling a business. Without a strong connection between leadership strategies and on-the-ground realities, even the most promising startups can find themselves veering off course and facing dire consequences.

11. Closure of Operations in Tier 2 and Tier 3 Cities

As PepperTap faced increasing logistical and financial challenges, initial signs of struggle became apparent in its operations across Tier 2 and Tier 3 cities. The ambitious expansion strategy that aimed to establish a presence in smaller urban markets began to falter as the company encountered unforeseen difficulties in managing its supply chain and delivery logistics. The decision to shut down operations in these areas marked a significant turning point for the company, revealing the strains of its rapid growth and highlighting the challenges inherent in servicing less populated regions where demand was not as predictable.

The closure of operations in these non-profitable markets was primarily driven by a need to reduce operating costs and refocus resources on more viable urban locations. By scaling back in these smaller cities, PepperTap aimed to streamline its operations and improve its financial stability. This strategic pivot underscored the importance of aligning business expansion efforts with market realities, reinforcing the notion that rapid growth must be supported by sustainable operational frameworks. Ultimately, this decision reflected a broader industry trend where many startups must reassess their geographic and operational strategies in response to real-world challenges.

12. PepperTap's Decline

By early 2016, PepperTap began a full-scale rollback of its operations, signaling the onset of its decline. The aggressive expansion that had once characterized the company now transformed into a painful contraction as mounting challenges became insurmountable. With growing competition from established players like BigBasket and Grofers, coupled with persistent operational failures, it became increasingly clear that PepperTap's business model was unsustainable. The company found itself grappling with logistical inefficiencies and an inability to provide reliable service, leading to widespread customer dissatisfaction.

As the market dynamics shifted, PepperTap was forced to reassess its approach to the hyperlocal grocery delivery segment. The initial vision of rapid growth and market domination was overshadowed by the harsh realities of operating in a highly competitive environment where consumer expectations were rising. Operational setbacks, including delayed deliveries and inventory management issues, further exacerbated the situation, eroding the brand's reputation and driving customers away. Despite its initial success, the company struggled to adapt to the evolving landscape of the grocery delivery market.

In April 2016, the culmination of these struggles led to the announcement of PepperTap's shutdown. This decision marked the end of a once-promising venture that had aimed to revolutionize grocery delivery in India. The closure not only underscored the challenges faced by startups in rapidly scaling operations but also highlighted the necessity of aligning ambitious growth strategies with practical operational capabilities. PepperTap's decline serves as a stark reminder of the complexities involved in navigating the hyperlocal delivery space.

The announcement of the shutdown elicited a mixture of responses from the industry and stakeholders. While some viewed it as an inevitable outcome of poor management and strategic missteps, others reflected on the valuable lessons learned from PepperTap's journey. The company's decline resonated throughout the startup ecosystem, prompting entrepreneurs and investors to reconsider their approaches to growth, competition, and operational efficiency in an increasingly crowded marketplace.

13. Reasons for Shutdown

The shutdown of PepperTap can be attributed to several interrelated factors that culminated in its inability to sustain operations. One of the primary reasons for its closure was the failure to scale profitably while maintaining service quality. Initially, the company experienced rapid growth, attracting a significant user base drawn by the promise of convenient grocery delivery. However, as it expanded aggressively into multiple cities, the challenges of ensuring consistent service quality became increasingly apparent. Customers faced issues such as late deliveries, missing items, and unreliable inventory, which led to dissatisfaction and a decline in customer loyalty.

Logistical complexity in managing operations across various cities also played a crucial role in PepperTap's downfall. The company struggled to establish a robust logistical framework capable of supporting its ambitious expansion plans. Each new city brought unique challenges related to local supply chains, delivery routes, and warehouse management. As a result, operational inefficiencies became more pronounced, contributing to an inability to deliver a seamless experience to customers. This logistical disarray not only affected customer satisfaction but also increased operational costs, further straining the company's finances.

Another significant factor leading to the shutdown was PepperTap's heavy reliance on external vendors and grocers. While partnerships with local grocers initially provided a competitive advantage, the dependency on these external entities created vulnerabilities in the supply chain. Any disruption in vendor operations directly impacted PepperTap's ability to fulfill customer orders on time. As the company expanded, the difficulty in maintaining reliable relationships with a growing network of vendors exacerbated its operational challenges, leading to stockouts and delays that frustrated customers.

Moreover, the inability to manage high cash burn rates proved detrimental to PepperTap's sustainability. The company faced mounting operational costs, including logistics, warehousing, and marketing expenses, which quickly outpaced its revenue growth. As funds dwindled, the leadership team found themselves in a precarious position, forced to make difficult decisions regarding resource allocation and operational cuts. The lack of a clear path to profitability became evident, raising concerns among investors about the long-term viability of the business model.

As PepperTap continued to grapple with these challenges, it became increasingly apparent that its strategy of rapid expansion without a solid operational foundation was flawed. The disconnect between ambitious growth targets and the reality of operational capabilities led to a series of missteps that compounded the company's difficulties. Investors and stakeholders began to lose confidence as the company's once-promising trajectory faltered under the weight of its operational shortcomings.

In light of these compounding issues, PepperTap's leadership faced the harsh reality that the business could not sustain itself in its current form. The mounting pressure from competitors, coupled with internal inefficiencies, ultimately forced the company to rethink its approach. The lack of a sustainable business model and clear pathways to profitability made it impossible for PepperTap to continue operations without substantial restructuring.

By early 2016, the decision to shut down became unavoidable. The announcement sent shockwaves throughout the industry, as PepperTap had once been heralded as a trailblazer in the on-demand grocery delivery space. Its failure highlighted the vulnerabilities that startups face when scaling in a competitive environment, emphasizing the need for careful planning, operational efficiency, and financial prudence.

In retrospect, PepperTap's story serves as a cautionary tale for entrepreneurs and investors alike. The lessons learned from its rise and fall underscore the importance of balancing ambition with operational realities and the critical role of effective supply chain management in the success of hyperlocal delivery businesses. The company's inability to navigate these complexities ultimately sealed its fate, leaving behind valuable insights for future ventures in the rapidly evolving startup ecosystem.

Key Points

- **PepperTap's journey** illustrates the pitfalls of aggressive expansion in the hyperlocal delivery market, emphasizing the importance of sustainable growth strategies over rapid scaling.
- **The company's downfall** reveals the logistical challenges and inefficiencies that can arise when operational frameworks are not equipped to handle expansion, leading to customer dissatisfaction and financial strain.
- **PepperTap's attempt to compete** with larger players like BigBasket and Grofers highlights the difficulties of market entry when established competitors have better logistics and financial resources.
- **The hyperlocal delivery model** that PepperTap championed held potential but ultimately failed due to the company's inability to maintain cost control and operational efficiency during its expansion phase.

- **PepperTap's failure** offers valuable lessons for future entrepreneurs about the need for strategic planning, the dangers of over-expansion, and the importance of aligning growth ambitions with a solid operational foundation.

Chapter 3. The Rise and Fall of TinyOwl: Cash Burn and Service Failures

1. Introduction to TinyOwl

TinyOwl emerged in 2014 as a promising food delivery startup founded by five graduates from IIT Bombay. The core idea behind the company was to create a mobile-based platform that allowed users to order food from their favorite restaurants with just a few taps on their smartphones. The founders, Gaurav Choudhary, Saurabh Goyal, Harshvardhan Mandad, and two others, identified an opportunity to revolutionize the food delivery space in India, which was at the time a growing but fragmented industry. By integrating technology and convenience, they aimed to streamline food ordering and provide users with a seamless experience.

The launch of TinyOwl came at a time when Indian consumers were becoming increasingly comfortable with mobile technology and online transactions. With smartphones becoming more affordable and internet penetration expanding rapidly, the conditions were ripe for a mobile-first platform like TinyOwl to succeed. The startup tapped into the rising demand for convenience among urban professionals, students, and families who were looking for quicker, easier ways to access restaurant-quality food. This made TinyOwl's initial offering particularly appealing in metropolitan areas.

TinyOwl's unique selling proposition was its ability to aggregate a wide variety of local restaurants on a single platform, making it easy for users to discover new places to eat and order from them in real-time. Users could browse through menus, place orders, and track deliveries—all within the app. This approach was particularly innovative for its time, as it combined elements of convenience, variety, and real-time tracking, which set it apart from traditional food ordering methods like phone calls or direct restaurant websites.

In its early days, TinyOwl focused on creating a user-friendly interface that simplified the food ordering process. The app's design was sleek, intuitive, and easy to navigate, which helped attract a large number of early adopters. TinyOwl was quick to expand its restaurant partnerships in cities like Mumbai and Bangalore, offering users a wide selection of cuisines and meal options. This focus on user experience and variety helped the platform gain traction, particularly among the tech-savvy, urban demographic that sought convenience in every aspect of their lives.

The founders were strategic in positioning TinyOwl as more than just a food delivery app. They wanted it to become a key player in the growing food-tech ecosystem in India, with the potential to scale rapidly across cities and even evolve into new verticals, such as restaurant logistics and meal delivery. Early investors saw the potential in this vision, and TinyOwl soon attracted significant funding from venture capitalists eager to get in on India's burgeoning startup scene. This initial optimism set the stage for the company's ambitious growth plans.

However, while the idea was well-received, the company's rapid expansion into new cities would soon become a double-edged sword. As TinyOwl started to grow beyond its core markets, the cracks in its operational model began to show. Scaling up without the necessary infrastructure to support the increasing demand placed a strain on the company's logistics and service quality, setting the stage for the challenges that would eventually lead to its downfall.

Despite its promising start, TinyOwl's success was fleeting. The company's growth trajectory masked underlying operational issues, which became more evident as competition in the food delivery space intensified. As new players like Swiggy and Zomato entered the market with stronger logistics and better service models, TinyOwl found it increasingly difficult to maintain its early momentum. In hindsight, the company's aggressive expansion and its inability to manage growing demand were major contributors to its eventual collapse.

In summary, TinyOwl's journey began with high hopes and a solid business model aimed at transforming food delivery in urban India. The startup was poised to capture a significant share of the market, thanks to its innovative approach and early adoption by consumers. However, the company's rapid growth and operational inefficiencies would soon lead to challenges that it was not prepared to handle. The next segments will explore these challenges in greater detail, from financial mismanagement to logistical failures that ultimately led to TinyOwl's demise.

2. Initial Success and Rapid Growth

TinyOwl's initial success can be attributed to a combination of factors, including its innovative business model, early mover advantage, and strong backing from investors. The company quickly gained traction in Tier 1 cities like Mumbai and Bangalore, where urban professionals and students were looking for convenient meal solutions. TinyOwl tapped into this demand with an easy-to-use mobile app that allowed users to order food from a variety of local restaurants. The app's user interface was clean, intuitive, and highly functional, which made it appealing to a tech-savvy audience.

The startup's founders were strategic in their approach to growth. They focused on building partnerships with local restaurants, giving them access to a wide range of dining options. TinyOwl's business model was based on charging restaurants a commission for each order placed through the platform. This allowed the company to scale without having to invest in its own kitchens or delivery infrastructure initially. Instead, TinyOwl relied on the restaurant's existing delivery systems, which helped the platform grow quickly without significant upfront operational costs.

TinyOwl's early marketing efforts were aggressive and effective. The company offered significant discounts and promotions to attract new users, positioning itself as a cheaper and more convenient alternative to traditional food ordering methods. These promotions helped the app gain a large number of downloads in a short period of time. Users were drawn to the convenience of being able to browse menus, place orders, and track deliveries—all from their smartphones. The ease of use, coupled with the discounts, created a compelling value proposition for busy professionals and students who frequently ordered takeout.

In addition to consumer adoption, TinyOwl also saw strong support from investors. In its early stages, the company raised $28 million in funding from top venture capital firms, including Matrix Partners and Sequoia Capital. This influx of capital allowed TinyOwl to rapidly expand its operations and enter new cities across India. With the backing of these investors, the startup grew at a rapid pace, adding more restaurants to its platform and expanding its reach beyond Mumbai and Bangalore. The company's rapid growth and ability to raise significant funding signaled strong confidence in its potential.

TinyOwl's ability to secure funding also enabled the company to invest in technology and marketing. The startup focused on improving its app's functionality, ensuring that it could handle increasing traffic as more users began using the platform. Additionally, TinyOwl ramped up its marketing campaigns, targeting both users and restaurants with promises of convenience and increased business. These efforts helped the company grow its user base and expand its restaurant partnerships, further solidifying its position as a major player in the food-tech space.

However, as TinyOwl expanded rapidly, the company's operational model began to face significant challenges. The startup's reliance on restaurant delivery systems created inconsistencies in service quality, particularly as the platform entered new cities. Some restaurants were not equipped to handle the surge in orders that came through the app, resulting in delays and poor customer experiences. These issues, while minor at first, became more pronounced as TinyOwl continued to scale. The company's rapid growth had outpaced its ability to maintain consistent service quality.

In hindsight, TinyOwl's early success may have been its downfall. The company's rapid expansion created a sense of urgency to capture market share, but it did so at the expense of operational efficiency. While TinyOwl was able to attract a large number of users in its early stages, the platform's inability to manage the increasing demand ultimately led to its decline. The following segments will explore how these operational challenges, combined with financial mismanagement, contributed to TinyOwl's eventual collapse.

In conclusion, TinyOwl's rapid growth in its early days was fueled by a combination of innovative technology, strategic partnerships, and aggressive marketing. The company was able to secure significant funding, which allowed it to expand quickly into new cities and gain a foothold in the competitive food-tech space. However, the company's operational weaknesses would soon begin to surface, leading to growing pains that TinyOwl was ill-prepared to handle.

3. Business Model and Funding

TinyOwl's business model was built around a simple yet powerful idea: connecting users with local restaurants through a mobile app that streamlined the food ordering process. The company charged restaurants a commission on each order placed through the platform, which allowed it to generate revenue without having to invest in its own delivery infrastructure. This commission-based model worked well in the beginning, as TinyOwl partnered with a wide variety of restaurants, offering users plenty of options to choose from.

One of the key advantages of TinyOwl's business model was its low operational overhead in the early stages. By leveraging the existing delivery networks of its restaurant partners, TinyOwl was able to scale quickly without having to build out its own fleet of delivery drivers. This allowed the company to focus on expanding its user base and restaurant partnerships, rather than getting bogged down in the logistics of delivery. The platform's simplicity and focus on convenience made it appealing to both users and restaurants, which helped fuel its early growth.

TinyOwl's ability to raise significant funding played a crucial role in its rapid expansion. In 2015, the company raised $28 million from prominent investors, including Sequoia Capital and Matrix Partners. This influx of capital gave TinyOwl the resources it needed to expand into new cities, enhance its technology, and increase its marketing efforts. The company's rapid growth trajectory was seen as a sign of its potential to dominate the food delivery market in India, and investors were eager to back what they saw as the next big player in the space.

With this funding, TinyOwl embarked on an aggressive expansion strategy, entering new cities and rapidly onboarding restaurants to its platform. The company's leadership believed that the key to success lay in capturing market share quickly, before competitors could establish a foothold in the food-tech space. This belief drove TinyOwl to invest heavily in marketing and customer acquisition, offering significant discounts and promotions to attract new users. However, this focus on rapid growth came at a cost.

As TinyOwl expanded, the company began to experience the challenges that come with scaling a business too quickly. While its commission-based model worked well in the early stages, it became less sustainable as the company entered new markets. In many cases, the restaurants that TinyOwl partnered with were not equipped to handle the volume of orders that the platform generated. This led to inconsistencies in service quality, which in turn led to customer dissatisfaction. The company's rapid expansion had outpaced its ability to ensure that its partners could deliver on the platform's promise of convenience and efficiency.

TinyOwl's funding also fueled its marketing efforts, which, while successful in attracting users, contributed to the company's high cash burn rate. The startup spent heavily on advertising, promotions, and customer acquisition, offering deep discounts to users in an attempt to grow its market share. While these efforts helped the company gain a large user base in a short amount of time, they also drained its financial resources. TinyOwl's reliance on discounts to drive user growth meant that it was operating at a loss, with little path to profitability in sight.

In hindsight, TinyOwl's business model, while innovative, was not equipped to handle the company's rapid expansion. The platform's reliance on restaurant delivery networks, combined with its aggressive marketing spend, created a situation where the company was burning through cash without a clear path to profitability. As competition in the food-tech space intensified, TinyOwl found itself struggling to maintain its position, despite the significant funding it had received.

In conclusion, TinyOwl's business model and funding were both strengths and weaknesses. While the company was able to grow rapidly in its early stages, its reliance on restaurant partnerships and aggressive marketing created a cash burn problem that it was ultimately unable to overcome. The next segment will delve deeper into the financial challenges that arose as TinyOwl continued to scale without addressing its operational inefficiencies.

4. Cash Burn and Financial Mismanagement

As TinyOwl expanded rapidly across India's urban centers, the startup began to face significant financial challenges, particularly due to its unsustainable cash burn rate. Cash burn refers to the rate at which a company spends its capital, and in TinyOwl's case, the company was spending far more than it was earning. This issue became more apparent as the startup aggressively pushed for market dominance, focusing on customer acquisition at any cost. The startup offered deep discounts, ran expensive marketing campaigns, and expanded into new cities without ensuring operational stability. As a result, TinyOwl's finances became increasingly strained.

TinyOwl's decision to offer significant discounts to attract users played a major role in its cash burn problem. While discounts helped drive initial user adoption, they also reduced the platform's profit margins. TinyOwl was effectively subsidizing orders, which meant that every meal ordered through the app was costing the company money. This strategy worked in the short term, as it helped the company build a large user base quickly, but it was unsustainable in the long run. TinyOwl's business model relied on restaurants paying commissions on orders, but with such low profit margins, the platform struggled to generate enough revenue to cover its expenses.

The company's high marketing spend also contributed to its financial problems. TinyOwl invested heavily in digital and offline advertising, attempting to create brand recognition and build customer loyalty. Billboards, social media campaigns, and app store promotions were all part of TinyOwl's strategy to gain visibility in a crowded market. However, the cost of these marketing efforts quickly added up, further straining the company's resources. TinyOwl's leadership team believed that gaining market share quickly would lead to long-term success, but they underestimated the financial toll of these short-term efforts.

Another factor that exacerbated TinyOwl's cash burn was its rapid expansion into new cities. Entering new markets required significant investment in building relationships with local restaurants, hiring staff, and adapting the platform to local needs. While TinyOwl had initially succeeded in cities like Mumbai and Bangalore, replicating that success in other urban centers proved to be far more challenging and costly. The company's infrastructure was not robust enough to support its rapid expansion, leading to operational inefficiencies that further increased costs.

TinyOwl's leadership faced a difficult balancing act. On one hand, they needed to scale quickly to compete with other food delivery platforms that were rapidly gaining ground. On the other hand, they needed to control costs to ensure the company's long-term viability. Unfortunately, the company's focus on growth came at the expense of financial discipline. TinyOwl continued to spend heavily on user acquisition and expansion without addressing the underlying issues in its business model, such as its reliance on deep discounts and its dependence on restaurant delivery systems that were often inefficient.

Despite raising $28 million in funding, TinyOwl's cash reserves were quickly depleted. The company's high burn rate meant that it was spending more money than it was bringing in, leading to a situation where it was constantly seeking additional funding to stay afloat. Investors grew increasingly concerned about the company's financial health, particularly as competitors like Swiggy and Zomato were able to scale more efficiently. TinyOwl's inability to manage its finances effectively made it difficult to attract new investment, which further compounded its cash flow problems.

In response to the growing financial crisis, TinyOwl's leadership attempted to implement cost-cutting measures. This included scaling back some of its marketing efforts, reducing discounts, and streamlining operations. However, by this point, the damage had already been done. The company's reputation had been tarnished by its service failures, and many users had already migrated to competing platforms. TinyOwl's financial mismanagement had created a situation where the company was struggling to survive, even as it attempted to rectify its mistakes.

In conclusion, TinyOwl's high cash burn and financial mismanagement were key factors in its downfall. The company's aggressive push for growth, combined with unsustainable discounts and expensive marketing campaigns, drained its resources and left it unable to compete effectively in the food-tech market. Despite its early success and substantial funding, TinyOwl's failure to control its finances ultimately led to its collapse. The next segment will explore the operational and logistical challenges that further contributed to the company's decline.

5. Operational and Logistical Challenges

As TinyOwl expanded its footprint across multiple cities, the startup encountered significant operational and logistical challenges that severely impacted its ability to provide consistent and reliable service. While the company initially relied on restaurant partners to handle deliveries, this model became increasingly difficult to manage as TinyOwl scaled. Many restaurants were unprepared for the surge in orders that came through the app, leading to delays, incorrect orders, and an overall decline in service quality.

One of the major operational challenges TinyOwl faced was the lack of control over the delivery process. Unlike its competitors, such as Swiggy, which built their own delivery networks, TinyOwl relied on restaurants to manage deliveries. This meant that the company had little oversight over the quality and timeliness of the delivery experience. As the platform grew, this reliance on third-party delivery systems became a significant liability. Restaurants that were not equipped to handle large volumes of orders often struggled to meet customer expectations, leading to negative feedback and declining user satisfaction.

In addition to delivery issues, TinyOwl faced logistical problems related to inventory management and order tracking. Many of the restaurants partnered with TinyOwl did not have sophisticated systems in place to track inventory in real time, which led to situations where users would place orders for items that were no longer available. This mismatch between the app's listings and actual restaurant availability caused frustration among users, who would frequently receive calls from restaurants informing them that their orders could not be fulfilled. Such experiences eroded trust in the platform and contributed to its declining popularity.

TinyOwl's rapid expansion into new cities also created logistical bottlenecks. The company had grown too quickly without building the necessary infrastructure to support its operations. In cities where TinyOwl had newly launched, the lack of established relationships with restaurants and delivery partners led to inconsistent service. Additionally, the company struggled to maintain the same level of quality control across different regions, resulting in varying user experiences depending on the city. This inconsistency made it difficult for TinyOwl to build a loyal customer base, as users could not rely on the platform for a seamless experience.

Another issue was the challenge of coordinating between multiple stakeholders—customers, restaurants, and delivery personnel—without a streamlined system in place. TinyOwl lacked an efficient communication system that could quickly resolve issues like order cancellations, delays, or delivery errors. As a result, when problems occurred, they often went unresolved for extended periods, further damaging the company's reputation. In contrast, competitors like Swiggy had invested heavily in customer service and logistics, ensuring that any issues were addressed promptly.

TinyOwl's leadership recognized these operational challenges but struggled to implement effective solutions. The company made several attempts to improve its logistics, including introducing third-party delivery services in some cities, but these efforts were often too little, too late. By the time TinyOwl began addressing its operational shortcomings, its competitors had already captured a significant share of the market by offering faster, more reliable delivery options. TinyOwl's inability to scale its operations efficiently made it difficult for the company to compete in the fast-paced food-tech industry.

The operational challenges also took a toll on TinyOwl's relationships with restaurant partners. Many restaurants grew frustrated with the platform due to the volume of order cancellations, delayed payments, and miscommunications. These issues strained partnerships, and some restaurants eventually chose to leave the platform, further limiting TinyOwl's offerings to users. This created a vicious cycle: fewer restaurants on the platform led to fewer users, which in turn made it harder for TinyOwl to attract new restaurant partners.

In conclusion, TinyOwl's operational and logistical challenges were a major factor in its decline. The company's reliance on restaurant delivery systems, combined with its inability to manage orders and inventory effectively, led to widespread service failures that damaged its reputation. As TinyOwl expanded, these operational inefficiencies became more pronounced, making it increasingly difficult for the platform to compete with rivals that had built more robust logistics networks. The next segment will explore how these service failures impacted customer satisfaction and contributed to TinyOwl's eventual downfall.

6. Customer Service Failures

As TinyOwl expanded rapidly and faced mounting operational challenges, the quality of customer service became a significant pain point. One of the core expectations from a food delivery service is timely and reliable delivery. However, TinyOwl's reliance on restaurant partners for deliveries meant that the company had limited control over the customer experience. As the platform struggled to meet growing demand, service failures became increasingly common, leading to a surge in customer complaints.

A major source of frustration for users was the frequent delivery delays. Customers often found themselves waiting far longer than the estimated delivery times provided by the app. In many cases, deliveries were delayed by over an hour, leading to dissatisfaction, especially when compared to competitors like Swiggy and Zomato, which were known for their punctuality. The inability to ensure timely deliveries significantly eroded TinyOwl's reputation, as customers began to lose trust in the platform's reliability.

In addition to delays, incorrect or incomplete orders became a recurring issue. TinyOwl's system lacked the real-time inventory management tools necessary to ensure that restaurants only displayed items that were available. As a result, customers frequently received calls from restaurants informing them that their chosen dishes were no longer available or, worse, they received incorrect items altogether. This lack of coordination between the app and the restaurants created a poor user experience, further damaging TinyOwl's brand.

Customer support was another weak point for TinyOwl. When issues arose, whether it was a delayed delivery or an incorrect order, users found it difficult to get timely assistance. TinyOwl's customer service infrastructure was not equipped to handle the volume of complaints that came in as the company grew. Many users reported long wait times when trying to reach customer support, and in some cases, issues went unresolved altogether. In contrast, competitors like Swiggy had built strong customer service systems that quickly addressed complaints and ensured customer satisfaction.

The decline in customer satisfaction was reflected in the app's ratings and reviews. As service failures became more frequent, users began leaving negative reviews on app stores and social media, further hurting TinyOwl's reputation. The company, once praised for its innovative approach to food delivery, was now facing a growing chorus of dissatisfied customers who were vocal about their frustrations. These negative reviews made it harder for TinyOwl to attract new users, as potential customers were discouraged by the platform's poor ratings.

TinyOwl's leadership recognized the growing issue with customer service, but their attempts to address it were too slow and reactive. While the company tried to improve communication with restaurants and implement third-party delivery services in certain cities, these efforts were not enough to reverse the damage that had been done. By the time TinyOwl began making meaningful improvements, many users had already switched to competitors that offered a more reliable and customer-friendly experience.

Customer loyalty, a key factor in the success of any platform, was severely impacted by TinyOwl's service failures. As customers encountered repeated issues with delivery and support, they became less likely to return to the platform for future orders. This lack of repeat business was a significant blow to TinyOwl's growth, as the company had relied heavily on user acquisition without successfully retaining customers. Competitors like Swiggy and Zomato, on the other hand, were able to build loyal customer bases by consistently delivering on their promises of fast, reliable service.

In conclusion, TinyOwl's failure to deliver consistent customer service played a major role in its downfall. The platform's inability to ensure timely deliveries, coupled with poor customer support, led to widespread dissatisfaction among users. As customer complaints grew, TinyOwl's reputation suffered, making it difficult to attract new users or retain existing ones. The next segment will explore how TinyOwl's competition further contributed to its decline by offering superior service and logistics.

7. Competition from Swiggy and Zomato

As TinyOwl grappled with internal challenges, external competition from food-tech giants like Swiggy and Zomato intensified, further accelerating its decline. These two companies, which initially focused on food delivery, quickly outpaced TinyOwl by offering superior logistics, more variety, and a much more reliable customer experience. The rise of these well-funded competitors posed a serious threat to TinyOwl, which struggled to differentiate itself in a highly competitive market.

Swiggy's key differentiator was its decision to build its own delivery network from the very beginning. While TinyOwl relied on restaurant delivery systems, which were often inconsistent and inefficient, Swiggy took control of the entire delivery process. This allowed them to ensure timely and reliable service, something TinyOwl could not guarantee. Swiggy's investment in a fleet of delivery personnel, equipped with real-time tracking technology, created a much smoother and more predictable customer experience. As a result, Swiggy quickly became known for its fast and efficient deliveries, which helped the platform build a loyal customer base.

Similarly, Zomato, which initially started as a restaurant discovery platform, made a strategic pivot into food delivery. Leveraging its established brand and extensive restaurant partnerships, Zomato rapidly expanded its delivery services. The platform already had a large user base, and the addition of delivery capabilities made it even more attractive to customers. Zomato's comprehensive restaurant listings, combined with a smooth food delivery experience, allowed it to dominate the market. TinyOwl, on the other hand, could not compete with Zomato's scale or established presence.

Both Swiggy and Zomato also excelled in offering variety, which was a significant advantage over TinyOwl. While TinyOwl had a limited number of restaurant partnerships, Swiggy and Zomato onboarded a vast range of restaurants, providing users with numerous choices across different cuisines and price points. This variety made their platforms more appealing to users, who could find whatever they were craving at any given time. In contrast, TinyOwl's limited options made it harder for the platform to retain users, especially as they sought more variety in their dining experiences.

Another area where Swiggy and Zomato outperformed TinyOwl was in user experience and app design. Both platforms invested heavily in creating intuitive, user-friendly apps that made it easy for customers to browse menus, place orders, and track deliveries. Real-time tracking was a feature that users highly valued, as it gave them visibility into when their food would arrive. Swiggy and Zomato offered seamless, efficient experiences that built trust with their users. TinyOwl's app, while functional, lacked many of these advanced features, which further contributed to its inability to keep up with its competitors.

Swiggy and Zomato were also more agile in addressing customer complaints and improving their services. Both platforms had invested in customer service teams that could quickly resolve issues related to orders, deliveries, or payments. This focus on customer satisfaction helped build brand loyalty and ensured that users had positive experiences, even when things went wrong. TinyOwl, on the other hand, struggled with customer service, which led to negative reviews and an exodus of users to more reliable platforms.

Funding was another area where TinyOwl fell behind its competitors. Both Swiggy and Zomato raised significantly more capital than TinyOwl, which allowed them to invest in logistics, technology, and marketing at a scale TinyOwl could not match. Swiggy, for example, raised over $150 million in its early rounds, giving it the financial firepower to expand aggressively and offer attractive discounts to users. Zomato, already a household name in India, had similar financial backing and could easily outspend TinyOwl in marketing and customer acquisition. This disparity in funding meant that TinyOwl could not keep pace with the rapid growth of its competitors.

As Swiggy and Zomato continued to grow, TinyOwl found itself in an increasingly precarious position. Users who had initially downloaded TinyOwl were now migrating to Swiggy and Zomato, where they could find better service, more variety, and a more enjoyable user experience. TinyOwl's inability to innovate or improve its logistics meant that it was quickly losing market share to these larger players. The company, which had once been seen as a pioneer in the food delivery space, was now struggling to stay relevant.

In conclusion, competition from Swiggy and Zomato was one of the key factors that contributed to TinyOwl's downfall. Both platforms offered superior logistics, a wider range of restaurant options, and a better overall user experience. TinyOwl, with its limited resources and operational challenges, could not compete with the scale and efficiency of its rivals. As a result, TinyOwl was gradually pushed out of the market, unable to keep up with the fast-growing food-tech giants.

8. Employee Layoffs and Internal Struggles

As TinyOwl's financial and operational challenges mounted, the company faced the difficult decision to downsize its workforce. In late 2015, just a year after its launch, TinyOwl announced layoffs, cutting around 300 employees from its workforce. This significant reduction in staff marked a turning point for the company, highlighting the severity of its struggles and signaling to the market that TinyOwl's future was in jeopardy. The layoffs, while necessary to reduce costs, also had far-reaching consequences for the company's internal culture and external reputation.

The decision to lay off employees was primarily driven by the company's high cash burn rate and dwindling financial resources. TinyOwl had expanded too quickly, hiring aggressively in anticipation of rapid growth. However, as the company's operational inefficiencies and service failures became more apparent, it became clear that TinyOwl was not generating enough revenue to sustain such a large workforce. The layoffs were a cost-cutting measure aimed at extending the company's runway as it scrambled to fix its operational issues and secure additional funding.

The layoffs, however, were poorly managed, leading to protests and public outcry. In particular, the situation in TinyOwl's Pune office garnered significant media attention when laid-off employees refused to leave the premises, demanding that the company's founders meet with them to discuss severance packages and compensation. The standoff between employees and management highlighted the growing frustration within the company and underscored the lack of clear communication from leadership. This incident further damaged TinyOwl's public image and contributed to the perception that the company was in disarray.

Internally, the layoffs had a devastating impact on morale. Many employees who remained with the company felt uncertain about their future, knowing that the company was struggling to stay afloat. The leadership team's decision-making was increasingly called into question, as employees saw their colleagues being let go without clear plans for how the company would recover. The sense of instability and lack of direction created a toxic work environment, with employees unsure of whether their efforts would ultimately save the company.

At the leadership level, TinyOwl also faced significant internal struggles. The company's founders, while passionate and driven, lacked the experience necessary to navigate the complexities of scaling a startup in a competitive market. As the company's financial situation worsened, the leadership team was forced to make tough decisions without a clear roadmap for recovery. This lack of experience in crisis management contributed to the company's inability to pivot effectively or develop a sustainable path forward.

The internal struggles at TinyOwl were further exacerbated by a lack of cohesion within the leadership team. As the company faced increasing pressure from investors and competitors, disagreements over strategy and execution became more pronounced. Some members of the leadership team advocated for doubling down on user acquisition through aggressive marketing and discounts, while others pushed for a more measured approach that focused on improving operational efficiency. These internal divisions made it difficult for the company to implement a unified strategy, which in turn hindered its ability to respond to external challenges.

The layoffs also had a lasting impact on TinyOwl's ability to operate efficiently. With a significantly reduced workforce, the company struggled to maintain the same level of service it had previously offered. Many of the employees who were let go had been responsible for managing restaurant partnerships, customer support, and logistics—critical functions that were already strained. The loss of these employees further weakened TinyOwl's operational capabilities, making it even harder for the company to compete with better-resourced rivals like Swiggy and Zomato.

In conclusion, the employee layoffs and internal struggles at TinyOwl were symptomatic of the larger issues facing the company. The decision to downsize, while necessary to reduce costs, was poorly managed and contributed to a loss of morale and public trust. At the same time, internal divisions within the leadership team made it difficult for the company to implement a cohesive strategy for recovery. These factors, combined with TinyOwl's external challenges, pushed the company further toward its eventual collapse.

9. Shutdown and Lessons Learned

By early 2016, it became clear that TinyOwl's attempts to recover from its financial and operational struggles were not enough to save the company. Despite multiple rounds of funding, aggressive marketing efforts, and attempts to improve logistics, TinyOwl was unable to compete effectively in the crowded food-tech market. The company's high cash burn, coupled with service failures and internal strife, left it with little choice but to shut down its operations. In April 2016, TinyOwl officially ceased operations, marking the end of one of India's early food delivery startups.

The shutdown of TinyOwl was a sobering moment for the Indian startup ecosystem. TinyOwl had once been considered a promising player in the burgeoning food-tech space, with the potential to disrupt the way Indians ordered food. Its rapid rise and equally rapid fall served as a cautionary tale for other startups about the dangers of scaling too quickly without a sustainable business model. The lessons learned from TinyOwl's downfall would go on to inform the strategies of future food-tech companies in India and beyond.

One of the key lessons from TinyOwl's journey is the importance of financial discipline. While it is common for startups to operate at a loss in their early stages, TinyOwl's reliance on deep discounts and aggressive marketing created an unsustainable financial model. The company burned through its cash reserves too quickly, without establishing a clear path to profitability. Future startups learned from this mistake, recognizing the need to balance growth with financial sustainability.

Another important lesson from TinyOwl's experience is the critical role of logistics in the food delivery business. TinyOwl's decision to rely on restaurant delivery systems, rather than building its own network, proved to be a major weakness. As competitors like Swiggy and Zomato invested in their own delivery infrastructure, TinyOwl was left with little control over the customer experience. The importance of owning the logistics chain became evident, as it allowed competitors to offer faster, more reliable deliveries, which TinyOwl could not match.

Customer service was another area where TinyOwl's shortcomings became apparent. The company's inability to address customer complaints quickly and effectively led to a decline in user trust and satisfaction. In contrast, competitors that prioritized customer service were able to build stronger relationships with their users, leading to higher retention rates. TinyOwl's failure to invest in customer support ultimately cost it a loyal customer base, highlighting the importance of customer experience in the success of any platform.

Lastly, TinyOwl's story underscores the importance of leadership and decision-making during times of crisis. As the company faced increasing challenges, its leadership team struggled to implement a clear and cohesive strategy for recovery. Internal divisions, poor communication, and a lack of experience in navigating downturns all contributed to the company's inability to pivot or adapt to changing market conditions. Future startup leaders took note of the need for strong, decisive leadership in the face of adversity.

In conclusion, TinyOwl's shutdown was the result of a combination of financial mismanagement, operational inefficiencies, and competitive pressures. The company's rise and fall offer valuable lessons for future startups about the importance of financial discipline, logistics, customer service, and leadership. While TinyOwl may no longer exist, its legacy continues to shape the strategies of food-tech companies in India and beyond.

10. Impact on the Indian Startup Ecosystem

TinyOwl's rise and fall had a significant impact on the Indian startup ecosystem, serving as both a cautionary tale and a source of valuable lessons for entrepreneurs and investors alike. The company's rapid ascent, followed by its equally rapid decline, highlighted the challenges of scaling a tech-driven business in a competitive market, where operational efficiency and financial sustainability are critical for long-term success. TinyOwl's story became a reference point for startups navigating similar challenges in India's fast-growing tech landscape.

The food-tech sector, in particular, was greatly influenced by TinyOwl's journey. As one of the early players in the food delivery space, TinyOwl had paved the way for the development of more sophisticated platforms like Swiggy and Zomato. These companies learned from TinyOwl's mistakes and adapted their business models to prioritize logistics, customer service, and financial discipline. The lessons learned from TinyOwl's operational inefficiencies helped shape the strategies of future food-tech startups, many of which focused on building their own delivery networks and improving user experience from the outset.

TinyOwl's collapse also had a broader impact on investor sentiment in the Indian startup ecosystem. The company's rapid failure raised questions about the sustainability of the "growth at all costs" mentality that had dominated much of the early-stage investment landscape. Investors began to place greater emphasis on the importance of operational efficiency, profitability, and clear business models when evaluating potential investments. TinyOwl's experience served as a reminder that rapid user growth, while important, is not a guarantee of long-term success.

In addition to influencing investor behavior, TinyOwl's story also shaped the way future entrepreneurs approached scaling their businesses. Startups in India became more cautious about expanding too quickly without first ensuring that their operations could handle increased demand. The importance of building a solid infrastructure before pursuing aggressive growth became a central tenet for many entrepreneurs, who saw TinyOwl's experience as a warning about the risks of overextending a business too soon.

TinyOwl's downfall also contributed to a growing awareness of the importance of customer experience in the success of tech platforms. As competitors like Swiggy and Zomato invested heavily in improving logistics, user experience, and customer support, it became clear that these factors were critical to building a loyal customer base. TinyOwl's failure to prioritize customer service highlighted the need for startups to invest in building trust and reliability with their users, a lesson that has since been embraced by the Indian startup community.

Despite its failure, TinyOwl's legacy lives on as an important case study in the Indian startup ecosystem. The company's innovative approach to food delivery, while ultimately unsuccessful, helped lay the groundwork for the development of more successful platforms that have since dominated the market. TinyOwl's rise and fall continue to serve as a valuable reminder of the importance of balancing innovation with operational efficiency, financial discipline, and customer satisfaction in the fast-paced world of startups.

In conclusion, TinyOwl's impact on the Indian startup ecosystem extends beyond its failure. The lessons learned from its journey have shaped the strategies of future entrepreneurs and investors, influencing how they approach growth, operations, and customer experience. While TinyOwl may no longer be a player in the food-tech space, its story continues to resonate within the Indian startup community, serving as both a cautionary tale and a source of valuable insights for the next generation of innovators.

Key Points

- **TinyOwl's journey** highlights the consequences of rapid growth without a sustainable business model, especially in an industry with high operational demands like food delivery.

- **The company's downfall** emphasizes the importance of managing cash flow effectively, as TinyOwl's aggressive discounts and high marketing spend led to an unsustainable cash burn rate.
- **TinyOwl's reliance** on restaurant partners for delivery exposed the platform to logistical challenges and service failures, leading to customer dissatisfaction and declining user retention.
- **Competition from Swiggy and Zomato** further strained TinyOwl's ability to stay relevant, as these rivals offered better logistics, more variety, and a superior customer experience.
- **TinyOwl's failure** serves as a reminder of the importance of balancing growth with operational efficiency, financial discipline, and customer satisfaction in order to build a sustainable venture.

Satyam Tripathi

Chapter 4. The Rise and Fall of FranklyMe: A Social Media Experiment in Video Interaction

1. Introduction to FranklyMe

FranklyMe, launched in 2014, was a video-based social networking platform founded by Nikunj Jain and Abhishek Gupta. The platform was designed to bridge the gap between influencers, celebrities, and their audience through personalized video interactions. In an era dominated by text-based social media interactions, FranklyMe aimed to offer a unique, video-focused approach, allowing users to connect more intimately with their favorite personalities.

The core idea of FranklyMe was to create a space where users could directly ask influencers or public figures questions and receive video responses. This concept set FranklyMe apart from traditional social media platforms and made it appealing to both influencers and audiences seeking more authentic engagement. Users could ask questions through the app, and influencers would respond with short, personalized video messages, adding a personal touch to interactions.

The app catered to a diverse user base, including celebrities, politicians, and other public figures. FranklyMe gained early traction as users embraced the idea of more direct and personal communication with influential people. This was particularly appealing in India, where fan followings of celebrities and public figures are substantial, and fans crave more interactive experiences.

The platform also offered users the ability to follow others, create profiles, and engage with content beyond just video interactions, making it a comprehensive social networking site. Despite its innovative concept, FranklyMe faced challenges in maintaining its momentum, competing with larger platforms, and monetizing its services effectively.

At its peak, FranklyMe garnered attention from investors and media, securing initial funding rounds. The platform was seen as a promising player in the Indian social networking landscape, but over time, it struggled to sustain user growth, revenue generation, and operational stability, eventually leading to its decline.

2. Early Adoption and User Engagement

FranklyMe quickly gained early traction, particularly among younger audiences who were eager for a more direct and personal way to engage with celebrities and influencers. The platform's unique value proposition of allowing users to ask questions and receive video responses from public figures set it apart from traditional text-based social platforms like Facebook and Twitter. This novelty factor played a significant role in capturing the attention of users who were increasingly looking for more interactive and immersive digital experiences.

A key aspect of FranklyMe's early success was its focus on onboarding celebrities and influencers from various industries. By offering a platform where influencers could respond to fan questions in real-time through video, FranklyMe created an attractive proposition for public figures seeking to increase their fan engagement. Celebrities from the entertainment industry, sports personalities, and even politicians were some of the early adopters of the platform. Their presence helped create a buzz around the app, drawing in users who wanted to engage directly with these influential individuals. FranklyMe's early user engagement strategy revolved around organizing live Q&A sessions and events where celebrities would answer fan questions on video. These events were heavily promoted on social media platforms, generating excitement and driving user downloads. The app also provided a user-friendly interface that made it easy for users to navigate and interact with their favorite personalities.

To further drive adoption, FranklyMe targeted university students and young professionals by promoting its platform on campuses and through youth-centric digital campaigns. The app's appeal to younger audiences, combined with the availability of well-known celebrities, resulted in high initial user engagement and rapid downloads in the first few months.

Despite this early success, the platform's ability to retain users became a challenge over time. While users were excited about interacting with celebrities at first, the novelty began to wear off, and the platform struggled to introduce features that would keep users engaged for the long term. This decline in sustained user engagement ultimately became a key issue for the platform as it moved forward.

3. Funding and Initial Growth

FranklyMe secured $600,000 in seed funding from Matrix Partners, which provided the necessary financial support to enhance its platform and expand its user base. This initial investment marked a crucial milestone for the startup, allowing it to refine its technology and implement marketing strategies aimed at increasing user engagement. With this backing, FranklyMe aimed to establish itself as a leading player in the video-based social networking space.

The primary focus of the funding was to scale the platform by onboarding a diverse array of influencers from various sectors, including entertainment, sports, and lifestyle. The team believed that by diversifying their influencer pool, they could attract a wider audience and boost user engagement. This strategy was rooted in the understanding that users were more likely to join the platform if their favorite personalities were actively participating and responding to questions.

Alongside influencer onboarding, the startup planned to invest in technical improvements to enhance the user experience. The goal was to create a seamless and intuitive platform that would encourage users to spend more time engaging with content. These improvements included better video quality, enhanced user interface design, and features that would facilitate smoother interactions between users and influencers.

While FranklyMe experienced early growth among specific user demographics, such as college students and young professionals, it struggled to achieve widespread adoption. The platform attracted users eager for direct interactions with celebrities, but this excitement did not translate into a broader user base. Many potential users remained skeptical of the platform, either due to concerns about privacy or a lack of awareness of its unique offerings.

Despite the initial funding and growth strategies, FranklyMe faced challenges in retaining users over time. The novelty of celebrity interactions began to fade, leading to questions about the platform's long-term viability. The startup needed to find ways to engage users continuously and offer value beyond initial celebrity interactions. Without this sustained engagement, the potential for significant growth appeared limited, raising concerns among investors about the platform's future.

4. Competitive Market Landscape

The competitive landscape for FranklyMe was daunting, as it found itself up against established social media giants like Instagram, Facebook, and Twitter. These platforms dominated the social networking space, boasting millions of active users and extensive resources for marketing and development. FranklyMe aimed to carve out its niche by focusing on video-based interactions, but competing with the likes of these behemoths proved to be a significant challenge. Users had already established their social media habits, making it difficult for a newcomer to entice them to switch platforms.

One of the major hurdles for FranklyMe was its inability to differentiate itself significantly from the established platforms. While it offered a unique proposition by connecting users directly with influencers through personalized video interactions, this feature alone was not enough to sway users away from their preferred platforms. Instagram and Facebook were constantly evolving, adding new features that catered to users' interests, such as stories, live videos, and direct messaging. As a result, FranklyMe struggled to communicate a clear value proposition that set it apart from these competing platforms.

In addition to facing fierce competition, FranklyMe also dealt with the challenge of maintaining relevance in an ever-evolving market. Social media trends shifted rapidly, and platforms that failed to keep pace risked losing user interest. FranklyMe's focus on video content was initially appealing, but as trends changed and users gravitated toward other forms of content, such as short-form videos and live streaming, the platform had to adapt quickly. Failure to do so led to declining user engagement and raised questions about the platform's long-term sustainability.

Moreover, the social media landscape was characterized by shifting user preferences and behaviors. Younger users increasingly sought platforms that offered instant gratification, such as TikTok, which capitalized on short, engaging video content. FranklyMe's traditional approach to influencer engagement did not resonate as well with this demographic, causing the platform to miss out on potential growth opportunities. The team recognized that to remain competitive, they needed to innovate continuously and respond effectively to changing user demands.

The struggle to maintain relevance was compounded by the perception of FranklyMe as a niche platform with limited appeal. While the focus on influencers attracted a specific user demographic, it did not broaden the platform's appeal to a wider audience. Many users remained unconvinced about the platform's long-term viability and opted to stick with more established social media networks that offered a broader range of features and functionalities.

Ultimately, FranklyMe's challenges in navigating the competitive market landscape underscored the importance of differentiation and adaptability in the social media space. As the platform sought to establish itself in a crowded field, it became clear that a singular focus on influencer engagement was insufficient. A more comprehensive strategy that addressed user preferences and leveraged emerging trends would be essential for any chance of sustained growth and relevance.

5. Challenges with Monetization

FranklyMe faced significant challenges regarding monetization, which became increasingly apparent as the platform sought to establish itself in the competitive social media landscape. Despite moderate user engagement, the startup struggled to implement a clear revenue model that would sustain its operations in the long term. The absence of a solid monetization strategy raised concerns among investors and stakeholders, as the platform's financial viability depended on its ability to generate revenue.

One of the primary issues contributing to the monetization challenges was the lack of paid features or advertising options. While other social media platforms offered various avenues for monetization, such as sponsored content, ads, and subscription models, FranklyMe had yet to develop similar features. This deficiency hindered the platform's ability to leverage its user base effectively for revenue generation, creating a disconnect between user engagement and financial sustainability. The absence of such monetization channels left the startup vulnerable, as it relied heavily on user growth without any immediate financial returns.

Furthermore, FranklyMe's heavy reliance on investor funds exacerbated its monetization difficulties. The startup raised significant capital in its early stages, which created an illusion of financial stability. However, as the platform's growth stalled, the dependence on external funding became increasingly problematic. Investors began to scrutinize the platform's lack of a clear path to profitability, raising concerns about its long-term viability. This scrutiny led to pressures on the founders to devise a workable monetization strategy quickly, but the absence of viable options limited their ability to pivot effectively.

The challenges with monetization also stemmed from the need to balance user experience with revenue generation. Many users were drawn to FranklyMe for its promise of personalized interactions with influencers, but introducing paid features or advertisements risked alienating the very audience the platform sought to attract. Striking the right balance between user engagement and monetization became a delicate dance that the founders struggled to master. As a result, the platform found itself caught in a cycle of chasing growth without a clear vision for revenue.

Moreover, the competitive nature of the social media landscape heightened the urgency for FranklyMe to establish a monetization model. Competitors had already found ways to capitalize on their user bases, and FranklyMe's inability to do the same further highlighted its vulnerability. Users began to question the platform's long-term prospects, which made it even more challenging for FranklyMe to retain existing users and attract new ones. The lack of a sustainable revenue model ultimately raised doubts about the platform's ability to survive in a space dominated by financially successful competitors.

As time progressed, the absence of a coherent monetization strategy became a critical factor in FranklyMe's challenges. The platform faced mounting pressure to innovate and explore new revenue avenues while maintaining the core user experience that initially attracted its audience. However, with limited resources and mounting operational challenges, the founders struggled to envision a monetization path that aligned with their original mission.

The failure to establish a clear revenue model ultimately impacted FranklyMe's growth trajectory and contributed to its decline. Investors and users alike sought assurance that the platform could sustain itself financially, and the inability to deliver on that promise led to skepticism about its future. As the founders navigated these challenges, it became evident that without a solid plan for monetization, the startup's ambitions of becoming a major player in the social networking space would be severely hindered.

6. Operational Struggles and Scaling Issues

FranklyMe faced considerable operational struggles as it sought to scale its platform to meet growing user expectations and demands. The initial promise of a seamless video-based social networking experience quickly clashed with the realities of operational inefficiencies that arose during its expansion phase. As the platform sought to attract a broader audience, the founders realized that the underlying infrastructure was not equipped to handle the increased volume of users and video content, leading to a series of challenges that hampered growth.

One of the primary operational challenges stemmed from the complexity of managing video content. Unlike text-based platforms, video demands significantly more technical resources, including bandwidth and storage. FranklyMe's technical infrastructure struggled to keep pace with the volume of video uploads, resulting in frequent buffering, slow load times, and overall poor user experience. These technical shortcomings not only frustrated existing users but also deterred potential new users, which hindered FranklyMe’s ability to compete in an already saturated market.

Furthermore, the startup's efforts to scale were stymied by inadequate management practices. As the platform expanded, the need for a well-defined organizational structure became increasingly apparent. Without clear roles and responsibilities, teams struggled to coordinate efforts effectively. This lack of cohesion created silos within the organization, leading to miscommunication and inefficiencies. The founders recognized that the operational framework was not robust enough to support the ambitious growth targets they had set, which further complicated their scaling efforts.

In addition to internal operational issues, FranklyMe faced external challenges related to user acquisition. The platform's growth strategy lacked aggressive marketing initiatives that could drive user engagement and sign-ups. While early user adoption was fueled by the novelty of the platform, the initial buzz faded without sustained marketing efforts to attract new users. Competing against well-established platforms like Instagram and Facebook, FranklyMe's failure to secure a strong marketing presence meant it was often overshadowed by competitors who were more adept at capturing and retaining user attention.

The founders attempted to implement various marketing strategies, but these efforts were hampered by limited resources and funding. The startup's financial constraints made it difficult to invest in large-scale marketing campaigns that could have elevated brand awareness and driven user acquisition. As a result, the platform struggled to gain traction in a competitive landscape where rivals were investing heavily in marketing and promotions to expand their reach.

Moreover, the lack of a comprehensive growth strategy meant that FranklyMe had difficulty articulating its unique value proposition to potential users. The initial promise of personalized video interactions with influencers was not clearly communicated in marketing materials, which may have contributed to user confusion about the platform's purpose. Without a compelling narrative to draw users in, FranklyMe found it challenging to stand out in a crowded marketplace, resulting in stagnating user growth.

As operational struggles continued to mount, the pressure on the founding team intensified. They recognized that scaling a platform like FranklyMe required more than just user interest; it demanded a well-oiled operational machine capable of supporting a growing user base. However, the internal inefficiencies and lack of a coherent scaling strategy left the founders scrambling to address issues that should have been prioritized during the initial growth phase.

Ultimately, the operational struggles and scaling issues faced by FranklyMe contributed to its challenges in establishing a sustainable presence in the social networking arena. The inability to effectively manage the technical demands of video content, coupled with a lack of aggressive marketing efforts, stunted the platform's growth and limited its potential for success. As the founders reflected on their journey, it became evident that a stronger focus on operational excellence and user acquisition strategies would have been essential for navigating the complexities of scaling a startup.

7. User Retention Problems

User retention emerged as a significant challenge for FranklyMe as the platform grappled with maintaining engagement levels among its initial user base. Despite a promising start, the platform faced a high drop-off rate soon after users signed up, indicating that the initial excitement surrounding the app did not translate into sustained engagement. This issue raised concerns about the platform's long-term viability and its ability to compete in the crowded social networking space.

One of the primary reasons for the high drop-off rate was the lack of content diversity on the platform. Initially, the allure of engaging with celebrities through personalized video interactions attracted users. However, as time went on, users began to seek more varied content offerings. FranklyMe’s narrow focus on celebrity interactions limited the breadth of content available, leading to user dissatisfaction. As users found themselves engaging with similar types of content repeatedly, they grew bored and less inclined to return to the app regularly.

Additionally, the platform struggled to implement features that would encourage long-term user engagement. While the initial concept of personalized video interactions was appealing, the absence of additional functionalities hindered the platform's ability to foster a vibrant user community. Users increasingly sought more interactive elements, such as live Q&A sessions, user-generated content, or collaborative features that would make their experience more dynamic. The failure to introduce such features led to a sense of stagnation, further contributing to the decline in user interest.

As the user base began to dwindle, growing dissatisfaction with the platform's features became apparent. Users took to app stores to express their frustrations, leading to a decline in overall ratings. Negative reviews highlighted issues such as slow load times, frequent crashes, and a lack of engaging content. This feedback reflected the overall sentiment of a user base that felt let down by a platform that had not evolved to meet their expectations. As app ratings dropped, it became increasingly challenging for FranklyMe to attract new users, compounding the retention issues.

Moreover, the lack of a feedback mechanism to understand user preferences hindered FranklyMe's ability to address retention challenges effectively. Without a clear understanding of why users were leaving, the founders struggled to implement changes that could reinvigorate the platform. The absence of user surveys or engagement analytics meant that critical insights about user behavior and preferences were overlooked, leaving the team with limited guidance on how to improve the overall experience.

The combination of limited content, insufficient feature development, and negative user feedback created a vicious cycle for FranklyMe. As users left the platform, it became more difficult to attract new users who were skeptical of the app's longevity and relevance. This downward spiral made it challenging for FranklyMe to regain momentum and build a loyal user base.

To combat these user retention issues, the founders attempted to re-engage users through marketing campaigns and promotional efforts. However, these initiatives were often met with lukewarm responses as users had already experienced the limitations of the platform. This indicated that mere promotional efforts would not suffice; substantive changes were necessary to revitalize user interest and encourage long-term loyalty.

In summary, user retention problems plagued FranklyMe as it struggled to keep its initial user base engaged. High drop-off rates, limited content diversity, and growing dissatisfaction with the platform's features contributed to a decline in user interest and app ratings. Without effective strategies to address these challenges, FranklyMe faced an uphill battle in establishing a sustainable presence in the competitive social networking landscape.

8. Investor Concerns and Pressure

As FranklyMe progressed through its initial growth phase, investor concerns began to mount due to the platform's inability to establish a clear path to profitability. While the platform initially captured the interest of investors with its innovative concept of personalized video interactions, the lack of a solid monetization strategy soon became apparent. Investors expect startups to develop viable revenue models, and the absence of such a framework raised red flags about FranklyMe's long-term sustainability.

The founders faced increasing pressure from investors to articulate a comprehensive monetization strategy. Investors sought clarity on how the platform intended to generate revenue, particularly given the substantial funds already injected into the startup. Without a definitive plan in place, investor confidence wavered, leading to heated discussions about the future of FranklyMe. Founders were urged to consider alternative avenues, including advertising partnerships, subscription models, or premium features that could create additional revenue streams.

As the platform struggled to maintain user engagement and retention, discussions about the viability of FranklyMe intensified. Investors began to question whether the platform could compete effectively in a saturated market dominated by established social media giants like Instagram and Facebook. The fear was that FranklyMe lacked the necessary differentiation to carve out a sustainable niche, leading to heightened skepticism about its future prospects.

The pressure on the founders intensified as investors demanded regular updates on user growth, engagement metrics, and potential revenue-generating initiatives. This scrutiny forced the team to reevaluate their strategy and pivot toward finding solutions that would appease their concerned investors. However, this pressure also led to a more reactive approach rather than a proactive strategy, leaving the founders scrambling to address investor demands without a cohesive vision for the platform's future.

Additionally, discussions about potential pivots created internal friction within the team. The founders had differing opinions on the direction the platform should take, with some advocating for a shift in focus while others wanted to stay the course. This discord made it challenging to present a unified front to investors, further eroding their confidence in the team's ability to lead the platform to success.

As concerns continued to mount, some investors began to distance themselves from the platform. The uncertainty surrounding FranklyMe's path to profitability led to reduced funding opportunities and a lack of interest from potential investors. The platform's reputation was at stake, and it became increasingly challenging to attract new investment without demonstrating a clear strategy for success.

In an attempt to quell investor concerns, the founders organized meetings and presentations to showcase the platform's user base and engagement metrics. However, these efforts often fell short, as investors remained unconvinced without a solid plan to translate user interest into revenue. The founders found themselves in a precarious position, caught between the expectations of their investors and the reality of a challenging market landscape.

Ultimately, the pressure from investors had a profound impact on FranklyMe's strategic direction. The need to appease investors led to rushed decision-making and reactive changes rather than a thoughtful, long-term strategy. As investor confidence dwindled, the future of FranklyMe hung in the balance, highlighting the critical role that financial sustainability and investor relations play in the success of startups.

10. Layoffs and Downsizing

In 2016, FranklyMe faced significant financial pressure that compelled the company to make the difficult decision to downsize its workforce. The layoffs, which impacted a considerable number of employees across various departments, were a direct response to the mounting operational costs and stagnant user growth that plagued the platform. As the company struggled to find a sustainable path forward amidst dwindling investor confidence, the decision to reduce headcount became a necessity rather than a choice.

The impact of these layoffs on employee morale was profound. Many remaining employees expressed feelings of insecurity and uncertainty regarding the future of the company. The abrupt downsizing created an atmosphere of fear and anxiety, as staff members questioned their job stability and the overall direction of the organization. This disruption in morale further complicated efforts to maintain productivity and focus on core business goals, ultimately leading to a decline in the quality of work produced by the remaining teams.

Public perception of FranklyMe also suffered significantly following the announcement of layoffs. Media coverage highlighted the company's struggles and painted a picture of instability, which deterred potential users and partners from engaging with the platform. Negative public sentiment can be particularly damaging for a startup that relies heavily on brand image and community engagement. As word spread about the layoffs, the perception of FranklyMe shifted from an innovative newcomer to a struggling entity on the brink of collapse.

Additionally, the layoffs created a ripple effect within the company, impacting its ability to innovate and respond to market demands. With a reduced workforce, the remaining teams faced increased workloads and pressure to deliver results without the necessary resources. This scenario hindered the company's capacity to explore new features or improvements that could have rejuvenated user interest and engagement. As a result, the company found itself in a vicious cycle of declining morale, diminished innovation, and further operational downsizing.

The failure to effectively communicate the rationale behind the layoffs to employees and the public exacerbated the situation. Many former employees expressed feelings of betrayal, as they had invested their time and effort into building the company. The lack of transparency regarding the company's financial situation and strategic decisions only fueled discontent among the workforce. This erosion of trust proved detrimental, not only in terms of employee retention but also in attracting new talent who may have been hesitant to join a company with such a tumultuous reputation.

In the wake of the layoffs, FranklyMe attempted to pivot towards more efficient operations and streamline processes. However, these efforts were often met with skepticism from both employees and the public. The lingering effects of downsizing created an environment where employees were reluctant to propose new ideas or take risks, fearing that any missteps could result in further job cuts. This reluctance stifled creativity and innovation, further limiting the company's potential for recovery and growth.

As the operational capacity of FranklyMe continued to shrink, the management team faced the daunting challenge of revitalizing the platform without adequate resources. The focus shifted towards survival rather than growth, resulting in an increasingly conservative approach to decision-making. This shift in mindset often led to missed opportunities, as the company became risk-averse in an already competitive market.

Ultimately, the layoffs at FranklyMe highlighted the fragile nature of startups and the complex interplay between financial health, employee morale, and public perception. The struggles faced by the company serve as a cautionary tale for other startups navigating similar challenges, emphasizing the importance of transparency, effective communication, and maintaining a strong company culture during times of crisis. As FranklyMe grappled with its diminished operational capabilities, the question remained whether it could find a way to adapt and thrive in an unforgiving landscape.

11. Shutdown and Lessons Learned

In 2016, FranklyMe officially shut down, marking the end of a promising venture that had once captivated users with its innovative approach to video-based social networking. The decision to cease operations came after a prolonged struggle to secure further investments, which ultimately highlighted the financial fragility of the company. Despite the initial excitement surrounding the platform, FranklyMe found itself unable to navigate the competitive landscape and deliver the value needed to attract and retain both users and investors.

One of the critical reasons for FranklyMe's failure was its lack of a clear revenue model. While the platform initially attracted a sizable user base eager to engage with influencers, it never established a sustainable way to monetize these interactions. The absence of paid features, advertising options, or subscription models left the company overly reliant on investor funding. This lack of financial self-sufficiency ultimately created a precarious situation where the company was unable to weather the storms of market fluctuations or shifts in user preferences.

Operational inefficiencies compounded the challenges faced by FranklyMe. The company's inability to effectively manage the technical demands of video content and scale its operations led to slow user acquisition and high drop-off rates. As a startup, FranklyMe struggled to create a seamless user experience that would encourage long-term engagement. This operational mismanagement not only hindered growth but also eroded the trust of both users and investors, further straining the company's resources.

The failure to scale was another significant factor in FranklyMe's downfall. As the platform aimed to expand its user base, it lacked the necessary infrastructure and strategic planning to support growth. Many startups often make the mistake of prioritizing rapid expansion over solidifying their core operations. FranklyMe's leadership faced mounting pressure to grow, yet they were unable to address the operational challenges that came with this ambition. This disconnect between vision and execution ultimately left the company unable to fulfill its potential.

Reflecting on the key lessons learned from FranklyMe's journey provides valuable insights for other startups. First and foremost, the importance of balancing user growth with financial sustainability cannot be overstated. Rapid user acquisition can be enticing, but without a robust revenue model to support ongoing operations, companies risk falling into a cycle of dependency on external funding. Startups must ensure that their growth strategies align with their financial realities to avoid facing similar pitfalls.

Additionally, having a clear revenue model from the start is vital for long-term success. Startups should proactively identify monetization strategies that are not only viable but also resonate with their target audience. This foresight can help create a sustainable business model that attracts investors and fosters trust among users. Failure to do so can lead to operational inefficiencies and hindered growth, as seen in the case of FranklyMe.

Moreover, the experience of FranklyMe underscores the importance of effective operational management in scaling a startup. Founders and leaders must prioritize building a strong foundation that can support growth and adapt to changing market dynamics. This includes investing in technology, streamlining processes, and cultivating a culture of innovation that empowers employees to contribute creatively to the company's mission.

Ultimately, the shutdown of FranklyMe serves as a cautionary tale for aspiring entrepreneurs and startup founders. While the desire to innovate and disrupt traditional industries is commendable, it must be balanced with practical considerations of financial sustainability and operational effectiveness. By learning from the mistakes of the past, future startups can better position themselves for success in a challenging and ever-evolving business landscape.

Key Points

- **FranklyMe's journey** highlights the risks of entering a saturated social media market without a clear value proposition, particularly when competing against established giants like Facebook, Instagram, and Twitter.

- **The platform's downfall** emphasizes the importance of having a clear revenue model from the start, as FranklyMe struggled with monetization and relied too heavily on investor funding without generating sustainable income.
- **User engagement issues** arose due to a lack of content diversity and limited differentiation from competitors, leading to low retention rates despite initial traction with influencers and celebrities.
- **Operational inefficiencies** and scaling challenges further hindered FranklyMe's growth, as the platform lacked the technical robustness required to handle video interactions at scale.
- **FranklyMe's failure** serves as a reminder of the importance of differentiation, a sustainable revenue model, and strategic execution in the highly competitive social media landscape.

Satyam Tripathi

Chapter 5. AskMe: Over-Expansion and Vendor Struggles in E-Commerce

1. Introduction to AskMe

AskMe was launched as an online marketplace aimed at bridging the gap between local businesses and consumers through a digital platform. Established in 2010 by Getit Infoservices, the platform sought to provide a comprehensive range of services, initially focusing on classified ads. This move capitalized on the growing trend of online shopping and the need for easy access to local goods and services.

The vision behind AskMe was to create a user-friendly platform that would empower both consumers and local vendors, allowing them to connect seamlessly. As internet penetration increased in India, the demand for such online marketplaces surged, prompting AskMe to expand its offerings beyond just classified ads. The initial concept laid a solid foundation for the platform's growth, targeting urban consumers who were increasingly turning to the internet for shopping solutions.

From its inception, AskMe aimed to cater to a diverse audience, including small businesses that could benefit from enhanced visibility. The focus was on creating a platform where local vendors could showcase their products and services, thereby increasing their reach to potential customers. This strategy not only benefited consumers seeking local products but also fostered a sense of community within the marketplace.

As the platform evolved, AskMe recognized the need to integrate e-commerce features into its offerings. The decision to expand into e-commerce came in response to market trends and consumer behavior, with an increasing number of users looking for convenient online shopping solutions. By incorporating e-commerce, AskMe aimed to enhance user engagement and attract a broader audience.

With a user-friendly interface, AskMe sought to differentiate itself in the crowded online marketplace. The platform's design emphasized ease of use, allowing customers to navigate through various categories and make purchases seamlessly. This focus on user experience played a crucial role in attracting initial users and encouraging repeat visits.

In the early stages, AskMe adopted aggressive marketing strategies to gain traction in the market. This included promotional campaigns aimed at highlighting the benefits of using the platform for both consumers and vendors. By emphasizing its unique selling points, AskMe aimed to position itself as a go-to destination for online shopping and local services.

The initial success of AskMe was characterized by rapid growth, particularly in urban areas where internet access was widespread. The platform quickly gained recognition among users seeking convenient shopping solutions, and its offerings expanded to include a variety of product categories. This growth trajectory set the stage for further expansion and diversification of services.

Overall, AskMe's journey began with a clear mission to provide a robust online marketplace. The combination of classified ads and e-commerce aimed to create a comprehensive platform that served the needs of both consumers and local businesses. As the platform continued to evolve, it sought to capitalize on the growing demand for online shopping in India, establishing itself as a significant player in the market.

2. Early Success and Market Position

AskMe experienced rapid growth in the e-commerce space shortly after its inception, capitalizing on the increasing demand for online shopping in India. This growth was driven by a unique positioning that appealed to both consumers and local businesses. By offering a platform that allowed users to access a wide variety of products and services, AskMe effectively tapped into the burgeoning e-commerce market, which was largely underrepresented at the time.

One of the critical factors contributing to AskMe's early success was its user-friendly interface. The platform was designed with the user experience in mind, making it easy for consumers to navigate and find what they were looking for. This ease of use encouraged repeat visits and fostered customer loyalty, essential elements in building a sustainable business. The intuitive design allowed users of varying technical proficiency to engage with the platform effortlessly.

To further boost its visibility and attract users, AskMe implemented aggressive marketing strategies. These campaigns were not only focused on traditional advertising methods but also leveraged social media and influencer marketing to reach a wider audience. By creating a buzz around its services, AskMe managed to position itself as a recognizable brand in the crowded e-commerce marketplace.

AskMe also focused on bridging the gap between local vendors and online shoppers, enabling small businesses to reach a larger customer base. This strategy allowed local sellers to showcase their products on a broader platform, helping them compete with larger retail chains. The inclusion of local vendors also contributed to the platform's appeal among consumers who valued supporting small businesses in their communities.

The integration of localized services into the platform played a significant role in attracting users. AskMe's emphasis on delivering products from nearby vendors ensured faster delivery times and a more personalized shopping experience. This local approach resonated well with users who appreciated the convenience and efficiency of receiving products from their community.

Another notable aspect of AskMe's growth was its focus on developing partnerships with various vendors, which enhanced its product offerings. By curating a diverse range of products from local sellers, AskMe created a marketplace that catered to the unique preferences of different consumer segments. These partnerships not only enriched the platform but also empowered local businesses to thrive in the digital age.

Customer engagement initiatives were also vital to AskMe's early success. The platform actively sought feedback from its users, allowing for continuous improvements based on their needs and preferences. By fostering a sense of community and actively responding to customer input, AskMe established itself as a customer-centric platform, further solidifying its market position.

Overall, AskMe's rapid growth in the e-commerce space can be attributed to its strategic focus on user experience, aggressive marketing efforts, and commitment to connecting local vendors with online shoppers. These elements combined to create a unique value proposition that resonated with both consumers and businesses, allowing AskMe to carve out a niche in a competitive market landscape.

3. User Acquisition Strategies

To attract users to the platform, AskMe implemented a variety of strategies designed to enhance visibility and engagement. The core of these efforts revolved around a well-defined marketing strategy that focused on reaching potential users where they lived. By targeting local audiences through community-specific campaigns, AskMe was able to create a sense of relevance and urgency, encouraging individuals to explore the platform.

One of the primary tactics employed was localized marketing campaigns. These campaigns utilized a mix of traditional media, such as newspapers and radio, as well as digital channels, including social media platforms. By customizing the messaging to resonate with the specific interests and needs of local populations, AskMe was able to foster a connection that transcended mere advertisements. This localized approach helped in building trust and rapport with potential users, making them more likely to engage with the platform.

Incentives played a crucial role in AskMe's user acquisition strategy. The company offered attractive promotional deals to early adopters, encouraging them to try the platform and explore its offerings. These incentives included discounts on first purchases, cashback offers, and referral bonuses for bringing friends and family onto the platform. By lowering the barrier to entry, AskMe successfully attracted new users who might have been hesitant to engage with a relatively unknown platform.

The referral program proved to be particularly effective in driving user growth. Existing users were incentivized to share the platform with their networks, creating a viral effect that amplified user acquisition efforts. This strategy not only rewarded current users but also expanded AskMe's reach into new communities and demographics, ultimately leading to increased platform adoption.

Additionally, AskMe collaborated with local influencers and community leaders to promote its platform. By leveraging the credibility and reach of these figures, the brand was able to establish itself as a trusted option within the local marketplace. Influencer endorsements provided a level of social proof that helped reassure potential users about the quality and reliability of the services offered by AskMe.

As user engagement began to grow, AskMe employed targeted digital marketing campaigns to further boost its reach. Online ads focused on specific demographics and interests, ensuring that marketing messages resonated with the intended audience. By analyzing user behavior and preferences, the marketing team could optimize campaigns to improve conversion rates and drive traffic to the platform.

Moreover, AskMe prioritized enhancing its user experience as a means of retaining new customers. The platform implemented feedback mechanisms that allowed users to voice their opinions and suggestions. This continuous improvement loop not only fostered user loyalty but also encouraged satisfied customers to spread the word about their positive experiences.

In summary, AskMe's user acquisition strategies revolved around localized marketing, attractive incentives, and collaboration with influencers. These efforts successfully attracted a diverse user base and created a community-centric platform that resonated with the needs and preferences of local audiences. The combination of targeted campaigns and user-focused initiatives laid a strong foundation for AskMe's initial growth in the competitive e-commerce landscape.

4. Expansion into New Services

As AskMe established itself within the e-commerce landscape, it recognized the necessity of diversifying its offerings to maintain growth and compete effectively with industry giants. To this end, the platform launched several new services, including AskMeBazaar, AskMeGrocery, and AskMePay. Each of these initiatives aimed to enhance the overall user experience by providing a comprehensive suite of services that catered to the evolving needs of consumers.

AskMeBazaar was introduced as a dedicated online marketplace where users could browse and purchase a wide variety of products from local vendors. This expansion into a more comprehensive retail environment allowed AskMe to position itself as a go-to destination for online shopping, bridging the gap between consumers and local businesses. By emphasizing local products and sellers, AskMe aimed to create a unique value proposition that set it apart from larger, more established e-commerce platforms.

In addition to retail, AskMe recognized the increasing demand for grocery delivery services. The launch of AskMeGrocery was a strategic move to tap into this growing market segment. By offering users the convenience of ordering groceries online and having them delivered to their doorstep, AskMe sought to enhance its relevance in the daily lives of consumers. This service not only expanded the platform's reach but also catered to the changing shopping habits of customers who preferred online grocery shopping.

Furthermore, the introduction of AskMePay aimed to create a seamless transaction experience for users across all services. By integrating a payment solution, AskMe sought to facilitate smooth and secure transactions, reducing friction for users while shopping. This feature positioned AskMe as a comprehensive platform where users could not only shop and order groceries but also manage their payments efficiently.

The combination of these new services represented an ambitious attempt to transform AskMe into a one-stop platform for all consumer needs, from shopping to food delivery and payments. This holistic approach aimed to increase user retention by providing multiple reasons for customers to remain engaged with the platform. As a result, AskMe's user base began to grow, attracting both new customers and retaining existing ones.

Geographic expansion was another critical focus during this phase of growth. As AskMe launched these new services, it simultaneously aimed to increase its presence in various regions. By targeting Tier 2 and Tier 3 cities, AskMe sought to capitalize on the growing internet penetration and smartphone usage in these areas. This strategy was designed to bring e-commerce closer to underserved markets and tap into the potential of new customer segments.

In addition to expanding its geographic reach, AskMe invested in localized marketing efforts to ensure that its new services resonated with diverse communities. By understanding the unique preferences and needs of consumers in different regions, AskMe tailored its marketing strategies to maximize engagement and adoption rates. This attention to local nuances further strengthened the platform's appeal among users.

In summary, AskMe's expansion into new services, including AskMeBazaar, AskMeGrocery, and AskMePay, showcased its commitment to becoming a comprehensive e-commerce platform. By diversifying its offerings and targeting specific market segments, AskMe aimed to build a loyal user base while establishing a significant presence in the competitive online marketplace. The company's strategic focus on geographic expansion and localized marketing played a vital role in facilitating its growth during this critical phase.

5. Over-Aggressive Growth Plans

In its pursuit of rapid growth, AskMe embarked on an ambitious expansion strategy that focused on penetrating Tier 2 and Tier 3 cities across India. This move was motivated by the recognition that these markets held significant untapped potential for e-commerce growth. With a burgeoning middle class and increasing internet access, these regions were seen as fertile ground for establishing a strong market presence. AskMe's leadership believed that capturing these emerging markets would enable the platform to outpace competitors and solidify its position in the industry.

However, the aggressive push into these new markets came with its own set of challenges. While the potential for growth was evident, the realities of establishing operations in less developed areas posed significant logistical and infrastructural hurdles. Many of these Tier 2 and Tier 3 cities lacked the necessary infrastructure to support rapid delivery and efficient supply chain management. As a result, AskMe faced difficulties in meeting customer expectations regarding delivery times and service quality, leading to increased customer dissatisfaction.

The pressure to compete with established e-commerce giants such as Flipkart and Amazon further compounded these challenges. These companies had already built robust logistics networks and brand recognition, making it difficult for newcomers like AskMe to gain a foothold. To compete effectively, AskMe felt compelled to invest heavily in marketing and infrastructure, often stretching its resources thin. This resulted in increased operational costs and a higher cash burn rate, creating additional financial strain on the company.

Furthermore, the aggressive growth strategy led to a lack of focus on core competencies. As AskMe sought to rapidly expand its services and geographic reach, it sometimes lost sight of delivering a quality user experience. The platform's early successes were built on strong vendor relationships and customer satisfaction, but the pressure to grow often meant that these foundational elements were sidelined. This shift in focus contributed to a decline in user engagement and retention.

The strain on resources was evident in various aspects of the business. Employee morale suffered as teams were stretched thin to manage the demands of rapid expansion. Internal misalignment arose as different departments struggled to coordinate their efforts, leading to inefficiencies and a disjointed approach to execution. The lack of experienced leadership in managing such a vast operation further exacerbated these issues, resulting in missed opportunities and operational missteps.

As AskMe grappled with these challenges, it became increasingly clear that its over-aggressive growth plans were unsustainable in the long run. While the ambition to capture emerging markets was commendable, the execution was flawed. The company needed to recalibrate its strategy, focusing on building a solid operational foundation before pursuing further expansion.

Ultimately, the combination of rapid expansion into Tier 2 and Tier 3 cities, pressure to compete with established players, and the strain on resources led to significant operational challenges for AskMe. These factors contributed to a decline in performance, highlighting the importance of balancing growth aspirations with sustainable operational practices. As AskMe navigated this tumultuous phase, it became evident that a more measured and strategic approach to growth would be essential for long-term success.

6. Vendor Relationships

Vendor partnerships played a crucial role in AskMe's business model, serving as the backbone of its e-commerce operations. These partnerships were essential for providing a diverse range of products and services to consumers, enabling AskMe to position itself as a comprehensive online marketplace. The platform initially focused on onboarding local businesses and sellers, which helped create a unique selling proposition by bridging the gap between these vendors and online shoppers. This strategy not only supported local economies but also contributed to AskMe's early success in establishing a competitive presence in the market.

In its formative years, AskMe experienced considerable success in building relationships with local vendors. By emphasizing the importance of these partnerships, the platform was able to offer a wide array of products, catering to the specific needs and preferences of regional customers. The onboarding process was relatively smooth, as many local businesses recognized the potential of an online marketplace to expand their reach and customer base. As a result, AskMe quickly gained traction, leveraging the trust and goodwill of its vendor network to attract users and enhance its offerings.

However, as AskMe continued to grow and expand its services, maintaining vendor satisfaction became increasingly challenging. The rapid scaling of operations put pressure on the platform's ability to effectively manage relationships with its vendors. Many local businesses began to voice concerns over delayed payments, inconsistent communication, and the perceived lack of support from the AskMe team. These issues not only strained vendor relationships but also led to a decline in trust among the very partners that had initially contributed to the platform's success.

The difficulties in maintaining vendor satisfaction were further exacerbated by the aggressive growth strategy that AskMe pursued. As the platform focused on expanding its user base and geographic reach, it often neglected the needs and feedback of its vendors. This oversight created a disconnect between AskMe's objectives and the expectations of its partners, resulting in dissatisfaction and frustration among local sellers. Many vendors felt that their contributions were undervalued, leading to a decline in their willingness to collaborate with the platform.

To address these challenges, AskMe needed to prioritize vendor relationships and implement measures to improve communication and support. Establishing clear lines of communication, offering timely payments, and actively seeking feedback from vendors could have fostered a more collaborative environment. By valuing and empowering its partners, AskMe could have strengthened its vendor network and enhanced overall satisfaction, ultimately benefiting both parties.

As the issues with vendor relationships escalated, they began to impact AskMe's reputation in the market. Negative feedback from vendors often made its way to consumers, tarnishing the platform's image and undermining its efforts to build a loyal user base. The dissatisfaction among local sellers not only hindered product availability but also affected the quality of service offered to customers. This cycle of discontent highlighted the critical importance of vendor relationships in sustaining a successful e-commerce platform.

In conclusion, while vendor partnerships were a foundational element of AskMe's business model, the company faced significant challenges in maintaining these relationships as it grew. The early success in onboarding local businesses was overshadowed by operational inefficiencies and a lack of attention to vendor satisfaction. For AskMe to achieve long-term success, it was essential to recognize the importance of nurturing these relationships and addressing the concerns of its partners. A more balanced approach that prioritized vendor satisfaction could have created a more robust marketplace, ultimately benefiting both AskMe and its vendor network.

7. Customer Feedback and Dissatisfaction

Analyzing customer feedback on AskMe's platform reveals a mixed bag of experiences, with significant concerns raised by users regarding its performance. Initially, the platform enjoyed positive reception due to its innovative approach to e-commerce and the convenience it promised. However, as the user base grew, so did the variety of feedback. Many customers expressed dissatisfaction with certain aspects of the platform, which pointed to critical areas needing improvement. The feedback served as a reflection of users' experiences and expectations, highlighting the discrepancies between what was promised and what was delivered.

One of the primary issues raised by users revolved around the platform's usability. While AskMe aimed to provide a user-friendly interface, many customers found navigation cumbersome and unintuitive. Complaints about complicated sign-up processes, difficulty in finding products, and challenges during the checkout process were common. Users expected a seamless and efficient online shopping experience, and when they encountered barriers, it led to frustration. This usability issue not only impacted user satisfaction but also contributed to a decline in repeat visits and overall engagement on the platform.

In addition to usability concerns, customers raised issues regarding the quality of service they received. Many users reported inconsistent delivery times, with delays becoming a frequent point of contention. The promise of quick delivery often fell short, leading to dissatisfaction among customers who relied on timely service. When users placed orders, they expected them to arrive within the stipulated time frame, and failure to meet these expectations undermined their trust in the platform. Such experiences negatively impacted AskMe's reputation and deterred potential new customers from choosing the service.

Another critical area of concern was the lack of effective customer support. Users reported difficulty in reaching out for assistance or resolving issues related to their orders. The absence of prompt and helpful responses from customer service representatives led to heightened frustration among users, who felt their concerns were not taken seriously. Effective communication and support are crucial for any e-commerce platform, and the shortcomings in this area further exacerbated the negative feedback from customers.

Furthermore, customer dissatisfaction often stemmed from unmet expectations regarding product quality. While AskMe aimed to provide a diverse range of offerings, users sometimes received items that did not match their descriptions or quality standards. Such discrepancies between customer expectations and the actual products received led to disappointment and diminished trust in the platform. Users sought assurance that the products they ordered would meet their needs, and when those expectations were not met, it contributed to an overall sense of dissatisfaction.

As customer dissatisfaction mounted, it became essential for AskMe to actively address these concerns. Implementing user feedback mechanisms and conducting regular surveys could have provided valuable insights into the areas needing improvement. By prioritizing customer experiences and actively seeking input, AskMe could have made informed decisions to enhance usability, streamline operations, and improve service quality. A commitment to addressing user feedback could have transformed customer dissatisfaction into loyalty and trust.

In conclusion, the analysis of customer feedback on AskMe's platform underscores the importance of usability, service quality, and effective communication in maintaining a positive user experience. While the platform initially garnered interest, the challenges it faced in these areas led to growing dissatisfaction among users. For AskMe to succeed, it was crucial to recognize and act on the feedback from its customers, ensuring that their experiences aligned with the expectations set by the platform. A proactive approach to addressing user concerns could have played a pivotal role in reversing the tide of dissatisfaction and fostering a more engaged and loyal customer base.

8. Shutdown of AskMe

The shutdown of AskMe in 2016 marked a significant turning point in the e-commerce landscape of India, a culmination of various financial struggles that had been brewing over the years. Despite its early promise and rapid growth, the company faced insurmountable challenges that ultimately led to its demise. Financial instability became a pervasive issue, with increasing operational costs and diminishing returns making it difficult for the platform to sustain itself. As the company's financial health deteriorated, it became evident that AskMe was unable to secure the necessary funding to keep its operations afloat, leading to the difficult decision to shut down.

The shutdown was met with widespread backlash, particularly from vendors who had partnered with AskMe. Many local businesses relied on the platform for sales, and the abrupt closure left them in a lurch, unable to recover unpaid dues. The financial mismanagement and failure to fulfill obligations led to protests from these vendors, who felt betrayed by the platform they had once trusted. Legal battles ensued as vendors sought compensation for their losses, highlighting the detrimental impact that AskMe's financial troubles had on its partner ecosystem.

The aftermath of AskMe's shutdown rippled through the startup ecosystem, raising concerns among investors and aspiring entrepreneurs alike. The failure of a once-promising platform served as a cautionary tale about the risks associated with aggressive growth strategies without a solid operational foundation. Startups began to recognize the importance of sustainable financial models and the necessity of balancing expansion with sound management practices. The challenges faced by AskMe resonated with many in the industry, prompting a reevaluation of strategies aimed at achieving rapid growth.

In the wake of AskMe's closure, discussions around the sustainability of Indian e-commerce platforms gained momentum. Investors became increasingly cautious, emphasizing the need for clarity in revenue generation and financial planning. The shutdown served as a stark reminder of the volatility that exists within the startup ecosystem, where even well-intentioned ventures could falter due to a lack of foresight and operational efficacy. The sentiment among investors shifted towards a preference for startups with robust financial strategies and proven market viability.

Moreover, the legal ramifications following AskMe’s shutdown created a climate of distrust among vendors in the e-commerce space. Many local businesses became wary of partnering with platforms that could potentially leave them vulnerable to financial instability. This skepticism hindered collaboration opportunities and strained relationships between startups and local vendors, impacting the overall health of the e-commerce ecosystem. The shutdown highlighted the critical need for transparency and trust between platforms and their partners.

In conclusion, the shutdown of AskMe in 2016 stands as a poignant chapter in the narrative of Indian e-commerce. It underscores the importance of sound financial management, the need for effective vendor relationships, and the risks inherent in aggressive expansion strategies. The consequences of AskMe's closure reverberated through the startup ecosystem, instilling valuable lessons that continue to shape the approach of new ventures as they navigate the complexities of growth and sustainability in a competitive market. The lessons learned from AskMe's journey remain relevant, serving as a guide for future entrepreneurs seeking to carve out their place in the ever-evolving landscape of e-commerce.

9. Lessons Learned from AskMe's Fall

The downfall of AskMe provides critical insights into the pitfalls of over-expansion, particularly when it lacks the necessary operational efficiency. One of the primary lessons from AskMe's experience is that rapid growth should be accompanied by robust systems and processes to manage that growth. Startups often feel pressured to expand quickly to capture market share and compete with established players. However, if the operational backbone is not strong enough to support this expansion, it can lead to inefficiencies, resource strain, and ultimately, financial instability. The failure to scale operations effectively can result in a loss of control over service quality, customer satisfaction, and vendor relations.

Another crucial lesson from AskMe's journey is the importance of maintaining strong vendor relationships. As a marketplace, AskMe relied heavily on its partnerships with local businesses to provide products and services to consumers. When the platform struggled financially, it failed to uphold its commitments to these vendors, leading to dissatisfaction and protests. Building and nurturing vendor relationships is vital for any marketplace, as these partnerships are foundational to a platform's success. Trust and transparency in these relationships can help mitigate risks and enhance collaboration, fostering a healthier business ecosystem. Companies should prioritize communication and support for their vendors, especially during challenging times.

Additionally, AskMe's fall underscores the need for sustainable financial models in e-commerce growth strategies. A startup may experience initial success and rapid user acquisition, but without a clear path to profitability, it risks financial ruin. AskMe's reliance on external funding without establishing a solid revenue generation strategy left it vulnerable when investments dried up. E-commerce platforms must prioritize the development of diverse revenue streams, whether through product sales, advertising, or subscription models, to ensure financial sustainability. A well-thought-out financial strategy can help mitigate risks and provide a safety net in times of economic uncertainty.

The lessons learned from AskMe's downfall resonate deeply in today's startup environment. Entrepreneurs must approach growth with caution, ensuring they have the operational capacity to support their ambitions. Moreover, fostering strong vendor relationships and creating sustainable financial models are integral components of a successful e-commerce strategy. The experiences of AskMe serve as a reminder of the complexities inherent in the startup landscape, where rapid growth can quickly turn into a downfall if not managed prudently.

In conclusion, the narrative of AskMe offers valuable lessons for entrepreneurs navigating the challenges of building and scaling e-commerce platforms. By learning from the mistakes of the past, new ventures can better prepare themselves to meet the demands of a competitive market, ensuring their sustainability and success in the long run. The importance of balancing growth ambitions with operational efficiency, strong vendor relationships, and solid financial planning cannot be overstated, serving as guiding principles for future entrepreneurial endeavors.

10. Future Outlook for E-Commerce in India

The challenges faced by AskMe significantly impacted the e-commerce landscape in India, highlighting the intricacies of operating in a rapidly evolving market. As startups and established players alike observed AskMe's decline, it became evident that the e-commerce sector is not just about technology and user acquisition but also about sustainable operations and solid business strategies. The lessons learned from AskMe's experience serve as cautionary tales for emerging businesses, emphasizing the importance of operational efficiency, customer satisfaction, and maintaining robust vendor relationships. This reflection on the past sets the stage for a more informed approach to future e-commerce ventures in India.

Despite these challenges, there remains a wealth of potential opportunities for new startups in the Indian e-commerce sector. The growth of internet penetration and smartphone usage continues to create a larger base of online consumers, particularly in Tier 2 and Tier 3 cities. Startups that focus on niche markets, personalized shopping experiences, and innovative service offerings can carve out distinct positions in this expanding market. The increasing adoption of digital payments and logistics improvements further enable startups to efficiently reach and serve their customers, opening avenues for specialized platforms that cater to unique consumer needs.

Moreover, the demand for localized products and services is on the rise, presenting opportunities for startups that can bridge the gap between local vendors and online shoppers. By building strong relationships with local businesses and offering curated shopping experiences, new entrants can differentiate themselves from larger players like Amazon and Flipkart. Focusing on community engagement and providing value-added services can create a loyal customer base and foster long-term growth. The emphasis on sustainability and ethical consumption is also gaining traction, paving the way for startups that prioritize environmentally friendly practices and transparency in their operations.

For sustainable growth in a competitive market, startups must consider several critical factors. First, developing a clear and adaptable business model that aligns with market dynamics is essential. This model should include diverse revenue streams, enabling flexibility in response to changing consumer preferences and market conditions. Additionally, focusing on customer experience and feedback will be paramount in creating products and services that resonate with consumers, ensuring repeat business and brand loyalty.

Second, startups must invest in technology and infrastructure that support scalability while maintaining quality. As seen with AskMe, operational inefficiencies can cripple growth, making it vital for businesses to establish robust systems and processes. Leveraging data analytics for inventory management, customer insights, and logistics optimization can help startups operate more efficiently and effectively.

Finally, fostering a culture of innovation and agility within the organization is crucial for navigating the evolving e-commerce landscape. Startups should encourage creative problem-solving and be willing to pivot based on market feedback. Emphasizing collaboration and communication among teams can lead to more innovative solutions and a more resilient business model.

In conclusion, the future outlook for e-commerce in India is filled with promise, provided that new startups learn from past failures and prioritize sustainable practices. The insights gained from AskMe's journey can guide future entrepreneurs in creating successful ventures that not only meet market demands but also contribute positively to the broader ecosystem. By focusing on operational efficiency, fostering strong relationships with vendors, and maintaining a commitment to customer satisfaction, startups can thrive in the competitive Indian e-commerce landscape. The evolution of this sector will continue to shape the way consumers shop and interact with businesses, and those who adapt will find opportunities to succeed.

Key Points

- **AskMe's rapid expansion** into multiple sectors, including e-commerce, grocery, and payments, stretched its resources too thin, leading to operational inefficiencies and cash flow problems.
- **Vendor payment issues** were a major factor in AskMe's downfall, as delayed payments damaged relationships with local businesses and vendors, ultimately leading to a loss of trust and service disruptions.
- **Competition from larger e-commerce players** like Flipkart and Amazon intensified pressure on AskMe, which struggled to keep up with better-funded and more efficiently managed competitors.
- **Internal management struggles** and misalignment of business priorities contributed to poor decision-making, further weakening the company's ability to recover from its financial and operational difficulties.
- **AskMe's failure** underscores the dangers of over-expansion without operational efficiency, the importance of maintaining strong vendor relationships, and the need for sustainable financial models in e-commerce ventures.

Satyam Tripathi

Chapter 6. The Rise and Fall of Dazo: A Struggle for Differentiation in the Food Delivery Market

1. Introduction to Dazo

Dazo, a food delivery startup founded in 2015, entered the market with the vision of simplifying the meal delivery process for urban consumers. The idea behind Dazo was to offer curated meal options, eliminating the overwhelming number of choices typically found on larger platforms like Swiggy or Zomato. The founders sought to create a platform that made food ordering quick and easy, particularly for busy professionals and students who valued convenience and efficiency.

The concept of Dazo revolved around offering a daily rotating menu with a limited selection of meals, curated from partner restaurants and cloud kitchens. By offering a smaller, pre-selected menu, Dazo aimed to optimize delivery times and simplify the decision-making process for users. This unique approach allowed customers to skip the often time-consuming process of browsing through extensive menus, making it an attractive option for those who needed a fast and hassle-free food delivery experience.

At its core, Dazo's founders were driven by the goal of addressing the growing demand for affordable, quick meal solutions in India's urban centers. With the rise of the on-demand economy, food delivery services were rapidly gaining traction, particularly in cities like Bangalore, where the hustle and bustle of city life left many people without the time or inclination to cook at home. Dazo sought to fill this gap by offering a reliable, curated service that catered specifically to the fast-paced lifestyles of urban dwellers.

The startup's strategy was to focus on quality over quantity by partnering with select restaurants and ensuring that the meals offered were of high quality and available at an affordable price. This emphasis on curation aimed to distinguish Dazo from larger food delivery platforms that provided a wide variety of options but often lacked consistency in meal quality. By narrowing its focus, Dazo hoped to build a loyal customer base that appreciated the simplicity and efficiency of the platform.

In its early days, Dazo enjoyed some initial success by capitalizing on the growing demand for quick and easy meal delivery. Its user-friendly app and curated offerings attracted a niche group of consumers who valued the limited menu options and the convenience they provided. For busy professionals and students, the ability to quickly order a meal without having to sift through numerous options was a major draw.

The company's founders believed that by eliminating complexity, they could carve out a unique space in the increasingly crowded food delivery market. They aimed to establish Dazo as the go-to platform for consumers seeking affordable, high-quality meals without the hassle of navigating extensive menus. This positioning, they hoped, would appeal to a segment of the market that was underserved by the broader, variety-driven platforms.

However, while Dazo's streamlined approach to food delivery had its advantages, it also came with significant challenges. The limited menu, which was initially a selling point, would later become a limiting factor as customer expectations evolved. Nonetheless, at the time of its launch, Dazo's founders were confident that their curated approach would set them apart in an increasingly competitive market.

In summary, Dazo was founded with a clear mission: to simplify the food delivery experience for urban consumers by offering curated meal options. With its focus on affordability, convenience, and quality, the platform initially resonated with its target audience. However, as competition intensified and customer demands shifted, the company would face growing challenges that would ultimately shape its trajectory in the food delivery landscape.

2. Early Market Position and Target Audience

Dazo quickly identified its target audience as busy professionals, students, and urban dwellers who were seeking quick, affordable meals in the fast-paced environment of major Indian cities. These individuals were often pressed for time, juggling their work and studies while managing their daily routines. For them, cooking was not always a viable option, and traditional food delivery services were often too time-consuming due to their extensive menus and variable quality. Dazo's streamlined approach to meal delivery aimed to address these pain points by offering a simplified, curated selection of meals, designed to meet the immediate needs of this demographic.

The platform's early success stemmed from its clear understanding of this target audience and its focus on offering limited but well-curated menus. By reducing the number of meal options available each day, Dazo eliminated the often overwhelming task of choosing from an endless variety of dishes, something that appealed to customers who wanted a quick and efficient meal delivery experience. This simplicity, paired with the promise of consistent quality, positioned Dazo as a convenient solution for time-strapped individuals who preferred a no-fuss approach to ordering food.

The curated menu approach also allowed Dazo to cater to specific dietary preferences and needs, such as vegetarian and non-vegetarian options, without overwhelming users with choices. This helped the platform stand out from other food delivery services that offered extensive menus but often lacked in terms of quality control and timely deleries. For Dazo's customers, knowing that they could order a reliable meal with just a few taps on their phones became a significant selling point.

The platform's traction was particularly strong in cities like Bangalore, where a large population of young professionals and students lived in urban centers with high demand for convenient meal delivery options. Dazo capitalized on the growing trend of food delivery in these urban environments by focusing on delivering high-quality meals quickly and affordably. This approach resonated with its target market, as many of these consumers were looking for cost-effective solutions that didn't compromise on taste or convenience.

Dazo's early marketing efforts were also geared toward attracting this specific demographic. The company leveraged digital marketing channels, such as social media and app-based promotions, to reach its target audience where they spent most of their time. By focusing on tech-savvy urbanites who were already familiar with mobile apps and on-demand services, Dazo was able to build a user base that appreciated the ease and simplicity of its offering.

Word-of-mouth also played a key role in Dazo's early growth. Satisfied customers who enjoyed the simplicity of the platform and the convenience of curated meals shared their positive experiences with friends and colleagues. This organic growth helped Dazo expand its reach within its target audience without relying heavily on traditional advertising campaigns. The platform's reputation for providing quick, reliable, and affordable meals spread rapidly among its core user base.

Despite its initial success, Dazo's limited menu also posed a potential risk. While the curated selection was an advantage in terms of operational efficiency and user experience, it also limited the platform's ability to cater to a wider audience with more diverse tastes and preferences. As competitors like Swiggy and Zomato offered increasingly larger menus, Dazo's simplicity began to lose its appeal for users seeking more variety and customization.

In conclusion, Dazo's early market position was built on its ability to cater to busy professionals, students, and urban dwellers seeking quick, affordable meals. The platform's focus on curated menus allowed it to attract a specific target audience that appreciated its simplicity and efficiency. However, as the food delivery market evolved and consumer expectations shifted, Dazo's initial strengths would later become challenges as it struggled to maintain its competitive edge in a rapidly growing sector.

3. Business Model and Service Offering

Dazo's business model was centered around offering a limited set of curated meals, sourced from partner restaurants and cloud kitchens. Unlike other food delivery platforms that prided themselves on providing extensive menus with countless choices, Dazo simplified the process by offering a streamlined menu each day. The core idea behind this approach was to offer users a few handpicked meal options, making the decision-making process quick and easy. This differentiation allowed Dazo to carve out a niche in the highly competitive food delivery market.

By curating meals, Dazo aimed to solve a common problem faced by many consumers — choice overload. With the overwhelming number of dishes available on larger food delivery platforms, users often struggled to decide what to order, leading to delays in placing orders.

Dazo's limited menu offered a solution to this by focusing on quality over quantity, giving customers a small but reliable selection of meals to choose from. This approach was especially appealing to busy professionals and students who wanted to avoid spending time scrolling through countless food options.

The curated meals were sourced from carefully selected partner restaurants and cloud kitchens, which ensured consistency in quality and taste. Dazo worked closely with these partners to ensure that the meals met a certain standard, aligning with the platform's promise of offering a convenient yet high-quality dining experience. This collaboration also helped Dazo maintain control over the types of meals it offered, ensuring that the menu remained simple and manageable.

Customers could choose from a fixed menu each day, with options that changed regularly to keep things fresh and engaging. This daily rotation added a layer of excitement for users, as they could look forward to new meal offerings without being overwhelmed by excessive choices. Dazo's menu typically included a few vegetarian and non-vegetarian options, catering to different dietary preferences without diluting the platform's focus on simplicity.

One of the key advantages of this limited selection was Dazo's ability to optimize delivery times. By offering a fixed number of meals, Dazo could streamline its logistics and ensure that deliveries were made quickly and efficiently. The platform's operational complexity was significantly reduced compared to other food delivery services that had to manage a large volume of orders for diverse dishes. This allowed Dazo to maintain a reliable delivery process, which was crucial for time-conscious customers.

Additionally, the simplified menu allowed Dazo to partner with cloud kitchens, which further enhanced its operational efficiency. Cloud kitchens, which operate solely for food delivery without the overhead of a traditional restaurant, aligned perfectly with Dazo's business model. These kitchens could prepare meals in bulk, ensuring that orders were ready for delivery in a timely manner. This partnership also allowed Dazo to offer meals at competitive prices, as cloud kitchens often operated with lower costs than brick-and-mortar restaurants.

The limited choice model, while efficient, also helped Dazo control its operational costs. With fewer menu items to manage, the platform could minimize wastage and optimize ingredient procurement. This operational focus on efficiency allowed Dazo to deliver meals at affordable prices, which was a key selling point for the platform. By reducing the complexity associated with managing a larger menu, Dazo was able to maintain lean operations while still delivering on its promise of convenience and quality.

In summary, Dazo's business model revolved around offering a curated, limited menu from partner restaurants and cloud kitchens. This model simplified the decision-making process for customers, optimized delivery times, and reduced operational complexity. While the curated approach provided Dazo with several advantages, it also limited the platform's ability to scale and compete with larger food delivery services that offered more variety. Ultimately, this model played a significant role in shaping Dazo's initial success but would later pose challenges as the company attempted to grow in a competitive market.

4. Initial Success and User Growth

Dazo experienced rapid user adoption during its early stages, particularly in metropolitan areas such as Bangalore, where the demand for convenient meal delivery was growing. The platform's simplicity and focus on curated meals resonated with urban consumers who were looking for quick, no-hassle meal options. This initial traction helped

Dazo carve out a niche in the food delivery market, attracting a dedicated user base that appreciated the convenience of the service. The early success of the platform was a testament to the founders' vision of providing a streamlined food delivery experience that saved time for its users.

One of the key factors behind Dazo's early success was its ability to identify and serve a specific target audience effectively. Busy professionals and students in fast-paced cities like Bangalore found the platform's limited, curated menu appealing. The simplicity of Dazo's offering, with its daily rotating options, eliminated the common pain point of decision fatigue that many users experienced when using larger food delivery platforms. This approach allowed Dazo to stand out from the competition, as customers knew they could quickly order a reliable, quality meal without having to scroll through an extensive list of options.

Early customers were drawn to the ease of use and convenience that Dazo provided. The platform's user-friendly app, paired with a selection of meals curated from trusted local restaurants and cloud kitchens, ensured that users felt confident in their food choices. By providing meals that were pre-selected for quality and taste, Dazo removed the uncertainty that often came with ordering from unfamiliar restaurants. This consistency in quality helped build trust among its users, encouraging repeat orders and contributing to the platform's rapid growth.

Word-of-mouth played a significant role in driving Dazo's early user growth. Satisfied customers shared their positive experiences with friends, family, and colleagues, helping to organically expand the platform's reach. The platform's simplicity and efficiency became a talking point among urban dwellers who valued convenience in their busy lives. This organic growth helped Dazo avoid the need for heavy marketing expenditure in the initial stages, allowing the company to focus on refining its operations and improving the overall user experience.

The growing demand for quick, no-frills meal delivery services also worked in Dazo's favor. As lifestyles in metropolitan cities became busier, consumers increasingly sought out time-saving solutions that offered convenience without sacrificing quality. Dazo's curated meal model aligned perfectly with this trend, positioning the platform as a solution for those who needed fast, reliable meals at affordable prices. The platform's ability to meet this demand further fueled its early growth, making it a popular choice for users who prioritized efficiency and simplicity.

In addition to individual customers, Dazo also attracted corporate clients who saw value in offering their employees easy access to meals during work hours. The platform's reliability and consistency made it an appealing option for companies that wanted to provide meal delivery services for their staff, especially in office environments where time was limited. This corporate adoption added another dimension to Dazo's growth, allowing the platform to expand its user base beyond individual consumers.

The success of Dazo's early growth was also supported by its partnerships with local restaurants and cloud kitchens. By collaborating with established food providers, Dazo ensured that it could consistently deliver high-quality meals that met its users' expectations. This focus on quality and reliability helped the platform maintain its positive reputation in the market, further driving user growth through word-of-mouth and repeat orders.

In summary, Dazo's initial success and user growth can be attributed to its focus on simplicity, convenience, and quality. By targeting busy urban consumers and offering curated meal options, the platform was able to rapidly gain traction in metropolitan areas like Bangalore. Positive word-of-mouth and the increasing demand for fast, no-frills meal delivery services contributed to Dazo's growth, helping the platform establish itself as a trusted solution for busy professionals and students in need of quick, reliable meals.

5. Market Competition and Rise of Competitors

As Dazo began to establish itself in the food delivery market, it quickly faced stiff competition from larger, more established platforms like Swiggy, Zomato, and Foodpanda. These companies had already built significant user bases and had the advantage of offering a wider variety of meal options. With their extensive menus, superior logistics networks, and aggressive marketing strategies, these competitors posed a serious challenge to Dazo's relatively simple, curated offering. Dazo's limited selection of meals, which had initially been a selling point, now became a disadvantage in the face of competitors who provided more choice.

Swiggy and Zomato, in particular, were expanding rapidly and building powerful brands that catered to almost every kind of food delivery need, from quick bites to gourmet meals. Their ability to partner with a vast number of restaurants across different price points meant that customers could order anything from budget-friendly fast food to high-end cuisine. In contrast, Dazo's small, fixed menu lacked this flexibility, which made it difficult to compete for a broader range of customers who wanted more variety in their meal choices.

Another critical factor that put pressure on Dazo was the superior logistics offered by these larger competitors. Platforms like Swiggy and Zomato had invested heavily in building out their delivery networks, ensuring faster delivery times and a more reliable service overall. Dazo, with its more limited infrastructure, struggled to match the logistical capabilities of these giants. In a market where speed and reliability are key to customer satisfaction, this disadvantage became a major hurdle for Dazo to overcome.

Additionally, competitors offered frequent deals, discounts, and loyalty programs that attracted cost-conscious consumers. Platforms like Zomato and Swiggy regularly provided users with promotional offers and discounts, making their services more attractive to price-sensitive customers. Dazo, on the other hand, did not have the same financial resources to offer such incentives on a large scale. This inability to compete on pricing further weakened Dazo's position in the market, as many users were drawn to platforms that offered them the best value for money.

The variety offered by these larger platforms also became a critical factor in user retention. As Swiggy and Zomato continued to add more restaurants and expand their offerings, customers were more likely to stay loyal to these platforms because of the sheer range of food options available. In contrast, Dazo's limited, curated menu no longer felt sufficient to meet the evolving demands of users who wanted more choices. This inability to provide variety ultimately impacted Dazo's ability to retain its users, who began to migrate to platforms that offered them a broader range of meal options.

Dazo also faced challenges in maintaining a consistent user experience. While it initially focused on quality and simplicity, the growing market competition required Dazo to innovate and expand its offerings, something that the platform struggled to do. Larger competitors had the resources to constantly improve their services, introduce new features, and enhance the customer experience. Dazo's relatively small size and lack of financial backing meant that it could not keep up with these developments, leaving it at a disadvantage in the fast-paced food delivery market.

In addition, the aggressive marketing strategies employed by Swiggy, Zomato, and Foodpanda put further pressure on Dazo. These platforms spent heavily on advertising, both online and offline, to maintain a strong presence in the minds of consumers. Dazo, with its smaller budget, found it difficult to compete with the widespread visibility and brand recognition of these larger companies. As a result, Dazo struggled to attract new users and retain its existing ones, further limiting its growth potential in an increasingly saturated market.

In conclusion, Dazo's inability to compete effectively with larger food delivery platforms like Swiggy, Zomato, and Foodpanda became a critical factor in its eventual decline. The limited variety of meals, weaker logistics network, and lack of aggressive pricing strategies made it difficult for Dazo to retain users in a highly competitive market. Despite its initial success, the rise of these larger competitors ultimately overshadowed Dazo's niche offering, forcing the company to confront the limitations of its business model.

6. Lack of Differentiation

One of the main challenges that Dazo faced during its time in the food delivery market was its inability to differentiate itself from the larger competitors like Swiggy, Zomato, and Foodpanda. Initially, Dazo's unique selling point had been its simplicity — offering a limited, curated menu to users looking for a quick and easy meal without being overwhelmed by choices. However, as the food delivery market evolved and customer expectations grew, what was once a strength for Dazo began to turn into a significant disadvantage.

Larger food delivery platforms continued to grow by offering wider menus, providing customers with countless options that suited every taste, budget, and dietary preference. These platforms could partner with a huge number of restaurants, giving users the ability to choose from fast food, gourmet meals, and even international cuisines. Dazo, on the other hand, maintained a fixed, limited menu that rotated daily, which no longer resonated with customers who were looking for more variety and customization in their meal choices.

As the market became more competitive, users began to prioritize flexibility when it came to food delivery. They wanted the freedom to order from different restaurants based on their changing moods and preferences. Dazo's curated menu model, while convenient in its early days, was too restrictive to satisfy these needs. The platform was not able to cater to customers seeking specific cuisines or dietary options, which limited its appeal as user preferences shifted toward more diverse food delivery experiences.

Another issue was the speed of delivery. While Dazo had optimized its operations to deliver quickly by limiting meal options, larger competitors such as Swiggy and Zomato were able to match and even exceed Dazo's delivery times due to their superior logistics networks. These competitors invested heavily in creating efficient, reliable delivery infrastructure, ensuring that customers received their meals quickly no matter where they ordered from. Dazo, with its smaller scale and fewer resources, struggled to keep pace in terms of delivery speed, which further weakened its position in the market.

The platform's simplicity, which had once been an advantage in reducing choice overload, now became a liability as users began to expect more variety from their food delivery apps. In an effort to stand out, competitors like Zomato and Swiggy introduced features such as customer ratings, live order tracking, and personalized recommendations, which further enhanced the customer experience.

Dazo, meanwhile, did not offer these additional features, making it harder to retain users who had come to expect a more robust, feature-rich service from food delivery apps.

The lack of differentiation in terms of pricing also hurt Dazo's competitive position. Larger platforms frequently offered discounts, deals, and loyalty programs that incentivized users to stay engaged and order more frequently. Dazo, which operated on a leaner business model, was unable to offer comparable discounts or loyalty rewards. This disparity in pricing strategies made it difficult for Dazo to compete with the heavy promotional tactics of larger players, particularly among budget-conscious customers.

Furthermore, the lack of innovation on Dazo's platform became evident as competitors continuously rolled out new features to enhance user engagement. While Swiggy and Zomato offered meal customizations, user reviews, and options for bulk ordering or party packs, Dazo's limited menu and rigid structure offered little room for personalization. This made it increasingly difficult for the platform to keep up with customer demands and market trends, leaving Dazo stagnant in comparison to its more agile competitors. In the end, Dazo's failure to evolve and differentiate itself contributed significantly to its decline. The platform had initially filled a niche for users who appreciated its simplicity, but as the food delivery market expanded, Dazo's lack of flexibility, variety, and innovative features prevented it from sustaining long-term growth. The food delivery landscape became more sophisticated, and Dazo's inability to adapt to these changes marked the beginning of the end for the platform.

In conclusion, the lack of differentiation was one of the key reasons Dazo could not compete effectively in the fast-evolving food delivery market. While its initial simplicity had helped attract early users, the rise of competitors offering more choice, faster delivery, and innovative features left Dazo behind. The platform's failure to evolve with changing customer expectations ultimately weakened its ability to retain users, leading to its eventual decline.

7. Operational Challenges

As Dazo attempted to scale, it began facing significant operational challenges, particularly in maintaining its partnerships with restaurants and cloud kitchens. Initially, Dazo's reliance on a few select partners allowed it to deliver consistent meal quality and fast service. However, as the platform expanded and customer demand increased, managing these partnerships became more complex. Ensuring that all meals met Dazo's quality standards while keeping up with the growing volume of orders proved to be a major challenge for the platform.

One of the key issues was managing the logistics of meal preparation and delivery. Dazo's model of offering a limited, curated menu was intended to streamline operations and reduce complexity, but as customer expectations for faster delivery times and higher-quality meals rose, the limitations of this model became more apparent. Partnering with multiple restaurants and cloud kitchens across different areas meant that Dazo had to coordinate deliveries from several locations simultaneously, often leading to delays and inconsistencies in service. The platform's small delivery network struggled to keep up with the demand, and this logistical inefficiency began to hurt its reputation.

Ensuring consistent meal quality also became an increasingly difficult task. While Dazo had initially established strong relationships with its partners, the process of maintaining the same high standards across various kitchens and restaurants proved challenging as the platform grew. As the number of orders increased, it became harder for Dazo to control quality at scale. Some customers began receiving meals that didn't meet their expectations, leading to complaints and dissatisfaction. This decline in quality control damaged the platform's credibility and made it harder for Dazo to retain loyal customers.

Delivery times, which had been one of Dazo's early advantages, started to suffer as the platform expanded. The combination of rising order volumes, a limited delivery fleet, and the complexity of coordinating deliveries across multiple locations led to delays. In a competitive market where companies like Swiggy and Zomato were consistently delivering faster due to their robust logistics networks, Dazo's inability to maintain fast delivery times put it at a distinct disadvantage. Customers who had once appreciated Dazo's quick and reliable service now found themselves waiting longer for their meals, further eroding the platform's appeal.

Another operational challenge was managing the relationships with partner restaurants and cloud kitchens. As Dazo scaled, it faced difficulties in keeping its partners satisfied, particularly when the platform's own operational inefficiencies started affecting them. Delays in meal pickups, issues with communication, and mismanagement of orders created friction between Dazo and its partners. This strained relationship with vendors meant that Dazo was at risk of losing the trust and collaboration it had initially built, further complicating its operational challenges.

The growing complexity of managing deliveries, quality control, and vendor relationships contributed to operational inefficiencies that Dazo was ill-equipped to handle. The platform's lean operational model, which had worked well in the early stages, struggled to adapt to the demands of a larger customer base. Without the resources and infrastructure to manage these complexities, Dazo found itself increasingly overwhelmed. Its inability to streamline operations while scaling only added to its woes as competitors continued to refine and expand their own systems.

As operational inefficiencies mounted, customer dissatisfaction grew. Delays, inconsistent meal quality, and poor communication about order status became recurring issues. Rising customer expectations, fueled by the success of larger platforms like Swiggy and Zomato, meant that Dazo's operational shortcomings were even more glaring. Customers who had once turned to Dazo for quick, simple meals were now turning to competitors who could offer faster service, more variety, and better overall experiences.

In conclusion, Dazo's operational challenges significantly contributed to its decline. The platform's struggle to maintain consistent meal quality, ensure timely deliveries, and manage its partnerships with restaurants and cloud kitchens became more pronounced as it scaled. These inefficiencies, combined with the growing expectations of customers, diminished Dazo's appeal and made it increasingly difficult for the platform to compete in a highly competitive market. The inability to address these operational issues in a timely manner ultimately weakened Dazo's ability to retain customers and grow.

8. Struggles with User Retention

As Dazo failed to differentiate itself from its competitors, user retention became a significant challenge for the platform. Initially, customers were drawn to Dazo's simplicity, enjoying the convenience of its curated meal options. However, as competitors like Swiggy and Zomato continued to expand their offerings and introduce more features, users began to expect more variety and flexibility in their food delivery choices. Dazo's limited menu, which had once been a strength, now became a limitation, as customers started gravitating toward platforms that provided a broader selection of meals and more personalized experiences.

Promotional offers and discounts provided by competitors further exacerbated Dazo's struggles with user retention. Platforms like Swiggy and Zomato frequently ran promotions, loyalty programs, and deals that attracted price-sensitive customers. Without the financial resources to match these offers, Dazo found it difficult to compete on price and incentives, which made retaining users even more challenging. Customers who had once appreciated Dazo's service were now lured away by the more attractive deals and promotions offered by larger players.

As customers began migrating to competitors, Dazo's ability to build a loyal user base was significantly affected. The platform struggled to maintain engagement, and without consistent users, it became increasingly difficult for Dazo to achieve sustained growth. While the initial user base had found value in the platform's curated approach, the lack of variety and evolving customer expectations led many to seek alternatives, leaving Dazo with a shrinking pool of loyal customers.

The platform's struggles with user retention had a direct impact on its overall growth. As the number of active users dwindled, Dazo's ability to scale and compete with larger platforms was severely hampered. Without a strong, loyal customer base, the platform faced increasing pressure to reinvent itself, but its limited resources and lack of differentiation made this difficult. Ultimately, Dazo's failure to retain users in an increasingly competitive market contributed to its eventual decline.

9. Financial Challenges

Dazo's financial challenges became increasingly apparent as the platform struggled to manage rising operational costs in an intensely competitive environment. The initial simplicity of its business model, which had helped the company streamline its operations in the early stages, soon became insufficient to support its growing user base and the demands of expansion. As operational inefficiencies mounted and Dazo attempted to scale, costs associated with maintaining partnerships, ensuring timely deliveries, and managing logistics began to spiral. These mounting costs, coupled with increasing competition, put the company under significant financial strain.

With limited funding compared to larger competitors like Swiggy and Zomato, Dazo faced significant challenges in scaling its operations. Unlike its rivals, which had raised substantial capital to improve their logistics, expand their offerings, and invest in customer acquisition, Dazo lacked the financial resources to make similar improvements. This lack of funding hindered Dazo's ability to enhance its services, introduce new features, and optimize its delivery operations, all of which were crucial to staying competitive in the rapidly evolving food delivery market.

Dazo's financial health further deteriorated due to its inability to secure additional investments. Potential investors were likely deterred by the platform's inability to differentiate itself and the growing dominance of larger, better-funded competitors in the market. Without the capital needed to scale and compete effectively, Dazo found itself unable to invest in crucial areas such as technology upgrades, marketing efforts, and logistical infrastructure. This lack of financial backing made it nearly impossible for the platform to keep up with the fast-paced demands of the food delivery industry.

As a result, Dazo's declining financial health became a significant factor in its downfall. The combination of rising operational costs, limited funding, and the inability to secure additional investments ultimately weakened the platform's ability to compete and grow. With no clear path to profitability and an increasingly difficult market landscape, Dazo's financial challenges contributed to its eventual collapse, marking the end of its brief tenure in the competitive food delivery sector.

10. Attempts to Pivot

As Dazo recognized the growing competitive pressure and its own operational limitations, the company explored options to pivot its business model in an attempt to regain traction. One of the key changes Dazo considered was expanding its menu to offer a wider variety of meals, addressing one of the primary complaints from users who desired more choices. Additionally, Dazo looked into offering more customized meal options to cater to specific dietary preferences, hoping this would attract a broader customer base. The goal of these changes was to provide a more flexible and engaging platform, one that could compete with the wide variety offered by competitors like Swiggy and Zomato.

Despite these efforts, Dazo struggled to keep pace with the larger players in the food delivery space. Swiggy, Zomato, and other major competitors had already built significant logistical infrastructures that allowed them to deliver meals quickly and efficiently across large regions. In contrast, Dazo lacked the financial resources and operational capacity to scale up in the same way. As a result, even with a more diversified menu, the platform couldn't match the reliability, speed, and variety of its competitors. This inability to compete on core service aspects continued to hinder Dazo's growth and user retention.

By the time Dazo attempted to pivot, the company was already facing declining user engagement and increasing financial strain. These attempts to introduce new offerings and cater to a broader audience came too late to significantly impact the platform's declining trajectory. The larger platforms had already solidified their presence in the market with better deals, faster deliveries, and more extensive customer bases. Dazo's late-stage pivots lacked the financial backing and strategic momentum needed to challenge these well-established competitors.

Ultimately, the pivot attempts were not enough to reverse Dazo's fortunes. While the company made valiant efforts to adapt to the changing demands of the market, it was unable to overcome the inherent disadvantages of its smaller scale and limited resources. User engagement continued to decline, and without significant improvements in its service offerings or financial health, Dazo could not sustain itself in the face of growing competition. These late-stage changes marked the company's final attempts to stay relevant, but they fell short of turning the platform around.

11. Shutdown of Dazo

In October 2015, just a few months after its launch, Dazo officially shut down its operations. The company, which had once aimed to simplify food delivery with its curated meal options, found itself unable to continue due to mounting financial difficulties and fierce competition in the rapidly evolving food delivery market. Dazo's inability to secure the funding it needed to scale, coupled with operational challenges and the rise of larger, well-funded competitors, forced the startup to make the difficult decision to close its doors.

The highly competitive market in which Dazo operated was one of the key factors that led to its demise. Platforms like Swiggy, Zomato, and Foodpanda had already established themselves as major players in the Indian food delivery space, offering wider variety, faster deliveries, and more attractive promotional deals. Dazo, despite its initial promise of simplicity and curated meals, struggled to differentiate itself from these giants. The company's limited menu and rigid business model, which had been strengths in the early stages, became liabilities as customer expectations shifted toward more variety and flexibility.

Dazo's leadership cited its failure to differentiate itself in a market dominated by larger platforms as one of the primary reasons for its closure. While the company had experimented with pivoting its business model by expanding the menu and attempting to introduce more customized options, these efforts came too late to have a meaningful impact. Dazo simply could not compete with the logistical infrastructure, financial resources, and customer engagement strategies of its competitors, leading to a steady decline in user retention and growth.

Financial difficulties also played a major role in the shutdown. As operational costs continued to rise, Dazo was unable to secure additional funding from investors who were increasingly hesitant to back a platform struggling to differentiate itself. The company had initially raised a modest amount of capital, but it was not enough to compete with the aggressive marketing and promotional campaigns of its larger rivals. Without the necessary financial resources, Dazo found it increasingly difficult to keep up with the demands of a growing user base and maintain the quality of its service.

The shutdown of Dazo marked the end of one of India's early curated meal delivery platforms. While it had initially captured the attention of a niche group of users who appreciated the simplicity of its offering, the rapidly changing food tech landscape in India proved to be too challenging for the company to navigate. Larger platforms continued to innovate and expand, leaving Dazo behind as customers gravitated toward more flexible and comprehensive food delivery services.

Despite its brief existence, Dazo's journey highlighted the challenges faced by startups in highly competitive industries like food delivery. The rapid growth of competitors, combined with shifting consumer expectations and operational difficulties, underscored the importance of differentiation and innovation in sustaining long-term success. Dazo's failure to adapt quickly enough to the evolving market ultimately led to its downfall.

The closure of Dazo also served as a cautionary tale for other startups entering the food tech space. It demonstrated that having a unique value proposition is crucial, but it must be backed by the ability to scale, adapt, and compete with larger players. Without the necessary financial backing, operational efficiency, and innovation, even promising startups like Dazo can struggle to survive in fast-paced, competitive markets.

In conclusion, Dazo's shutdown in October 2015 was a result of financial difficulties, intense competition, and the inability to secure a clear differentiation from its larger rivals. The company's vision of simplifying food delivery with curated meal options was promising, but the rapidly evolving food delivery landscape in India proved too difficult for the platform to navigate. Dazo's closure marked the end of its journey as one of India's early food delivery startups, serving as a reminder of the challenges and complexities of sustaining a successful business in competitive markets.

Key Points

- **Dazo's journey** highlights the challenges of entering a highly competitive food delivery market without strong differentiation, as the platform struggled to stand out against larger competitors like Swiggy and Zomato.

- **The platform's failure** to offer variety and flexibility limited its appeal, with Dazo's curated menu approach becoming a disadvantage as users demanded more choices and personalized experiences.
- **Operational inefficiencies** in managing logistics and maintaining consistent partnerships with restaurants contributed to service issues, which further impacted customer retention and satisfaction.
- **Dazo's inability to scale** its business effectively due to limited funding and a narrow target audience hindered its growth, leaving the platform unable to compete in a rapidly evolving market.
- **Dazo's fall** serves as a lesson in the importance of differentiation, operational efficiency, and flexibility in a crowded market, where innovation and user experience are key to long-term success.

Chapter 7. iTiffin: The Rise and Fall of a Health-Focused Meal Delivery Service

1. Introduction to iTiffin

iTiffin, founded in 2013, aimed to revolutionize the traditional tiffin service market by offering healthy, balanced meals tailored to the needs of working professionals, students, and health-conscious individuals. The startup emerged at a time when urban consumers were becoming increasingly health-conscious and looking for convenient ways to maintain a balanced diet amidst their busy lives. By offering meals curated by chefs and nutritionists, iTiffin sought to provide a solution that catered to individuals looking to maintain good nutrition without sacrificing convenience.

The company's vision was simple yet ambitious: provide customers with the kind of balanced, portion-controlled meals that would meet their dietary requirements. iTiffin was positioned as a premium meal delivery service that focused not just on convenience but on providing carefully curated, nutritious meals. This placed the company in a niche market that appealed to urban professionals and students who sought healthy options for their daily meals.

The startup quickly gained attention for its innovative approach to food delivery, which diverged from the usual calorie-heavy or fast-food-focused options in the market. iTiffin marketed itself as a service for people who cared about what they ate but didn't have the time or resources to prepare nutritious meals on their own. With increasing health awareness among urban dwellers, iTiffin's concept seemed poised for success.

Targeting customers who were not only looking for convenience but also concerned with maintaining a healthy diet, iTiffin tapped into a growing demand for health-conscious solutions in the meal delivery sector. The idea was simple: users could subscribe to meal plans tailored to their dietary needs and have fresh, healthy meals delivered to their doorsteps daily.

iTiffin's target audience included busy professionals in corporate settings, students living away from home, and fitness enthusiasts who wanted to control their calorie intake and manage their nutrition better. This was a market that had previously been underserved by food delivery services, which traditionally focused on quick, convenient, and often unhealthy options.

With its strong focus on nutrition, iTiffin differentiated itself by offering personalized meal plans designed to meet specific health goals. Whether it was weight loss, weight maintenance, or simply balanced nutrition, iTiffin aimed to provide meals that would support its customers' dietary objectives. This unique selling point helped the company stand out from other food delivery services in its early days.

The startup initially started its operations in Bangalore, one of India's major urban centers, which had a large population of professionals and students. Bangalore, with its bustling tech industry and high density of corporate offices, was the perfect testing ground for iTiffin's concept. The company hoped to expand its operations to other cities once it had perfected its model in Bangalore.

In conclusion, iTiffin's vision was to offer a unique blend of convenience and nutrition, targeting urban consumers who were looking for more than just fast food. By combining the expertise of nutritionists and chefs, iTiffin hoped to carve out a niche in the competitive food delivery market by focusing on health-conscious individuals who valued their well-being.

2. Early Market Success

iTiffin enjoyed early success in the market due to its unique positioning as a health-focused meal delivery service. The startup quickly gained traction among urban professionals, students, and fitness enthusiasts who were actively seeking healthier alternatives to traditional meal delivery options. The company's initial launch in Bangalore was well-received, as the city's growing health-conscious population resonated with the idea of receiving balanced, nutritious meals delivered directly to their doors.

One of the main drivers behind iTiffin's early success was the rising demand for healthy and convenient meal solutions. As lifestyles in urban areas became more fast-paced, people were increasingly turning to meal delivery services to save time while maintaining their nutrition. iTiffin was able to fill this gap by offering meal plans that were carefully curated and aligned with health goals, making it a popular choice among individuals who wanted to avoid junk food and calorie-laden options.

The startup's ability to connect with its target audience was instrumental in its initial growth. By offering meals that were designed by nutritionists and prepared by professional chefs, iTiffin positioned itself as a premium service. This attracted customers who were willing to pay a little extra for the convenience of receiving meals that were not only healthy but also customized to their dietary preferences.

iTiffin's early marketing efforts played a key role in spreading awareness about the brand. The company utilized digital platforms, including social media, to reach out to its target audience and promote the health benefits of subscribing to their meal plans. This digital-first approach helped iTiffin build a loyal customer base that appreciated the simplicity and convenience of ordering nutritious meals online.

Customer testimonials also contributed to iTiffin's early success. Satisfied customers shared their positive experiences with friends, family, and colleagues, which helped the brand grow through word-of-mouth. This organic growth was crucial in building credibility for the platform, especially in an industry where trust in food quality and service is paramount.

In addition to direct consumer engagement, iTiffin also explored partnerships with gyms and fitness centers to tap into the growing health and wellness industry. These collaborations helped the company reach a wider audience of fitness enthusiasts who were looking for meal solutions that complemented their workout routines and health goals.

By focusing on quality, customization, and health, iTiffin was able to differentiate itself from other meal delivery services that were primarily convenience-driven. This differentiation allowed the startup to establish itself as a leader in the healthy meal delivery space, particularly in Bangalore, where health-conscious consumers were actively seeking such services.

In conclusion, iTiffin's early market success can be attributed to its ability to fill a gap in the market for healthy, convenient meal delivery options. The company's focus on nutrition, coupled with its strategic marketing and partnerships, helped it build a loyal customer base and establish a foothold in the competitive food delivery industry.

3. Business Model and Service Offering

iTiffin operated on a subscription-based business model that offered customers a range of meal plans tailored to their specific dietary needs. Customers could subscribe to weekly or monthly meal plans, receiving fresh, healthy meals delivered to their doorstep daily. The subscription model allowed iTiffin to secure regular, recurring revenue, which was crucial for sustaining its operations and maintaining consistent customer engagement.

The company's service offerings were highly customizable, with meal plans designed for different health goals such as weight loss, muscle gain, or general wellness. iTiffin's meals were created by a team of nutritionists and chefs, ensuring that each meal was balanced in terms of macronutrients, portion control, and calorie intake. This focus on personalized nutrition gave iTiffin a unique edge in the meal delivery market, especially among health-conscious individuals.

iTiffin provided various meal plan options to cater to different customer preferences. These included vegetarian and non-vegetarian meals, as well as options for individuals with specific dietary restrictions or food allergies. This flexibility allowed the platform to appeal to a wider range of customers, including those with specialized dietary needs who struggled to find convenient meal options elsewhere.

The startup positioned itself as a premium service, offering meals that were both nutritious and delicious. Unlike traditional tiffin services, which focused primarily on convenience and affordability, iTiffin emphasized the quality of ingredients and the importance of balanced nutrition. This approach attracted customers who were willing to pay more for healthier meal options that aligned with their lifestyle and fitness goals.

iTiffin's subscription model provided convenience for customers who wanted to automate their meal planning and delivery. Once customers selected their preferred meal plan, they could sit back and have their meals delivered regularly without having to place new orders each day. This convenience factor played a significant role in retaining customers, especially busy professionals who had little time to think about their daily meals.

The company's commitment to providing personalized, nutritionist-approved meals set it apart from other meal delivery services that offered standard, calorie-dense meals. By focusing on health and wellness, iTiffin was able to tap into a growing market of consumers who were becoming more mindful of their eating habits and the impact of nutrition on their overall well-being.

In addition to individual meal plans, iTiffin also experimented with corporate meal services, offering customized meal solutions for companies looking to provide healthy lunch options to their employees. This allowed the company to expand its customer base beyond individual subscribers, bringing in corporate clients who were interested in promoting health and wellness in the workplace.

Overall, iTiffin's business model was centered on providing personalized, healthy meal options to health-conscious consumers. The subscription-based service allowed for consistent revenue, while the focus on nutrition and meal customization helped differentiate the platform from other players in the crowded meal delivery market.

4. Customer Experience and Growth

The early success of iTiffin was largely driven by its ability to deliver a high-quality customer experience. Customers appreciated the convenience of having healthy, balanced meals delivered straight to their homes or offices, saving them the time and effort of planning and preparing their own meals. This convenience, coupled with the company's focus on nutrition, attracted a loyal customer base that valued both health and time efficiency.

The level of personalization offered by iTiffin also played a key role in enhancing the customer experience. Unlike many other meal delivery services that offered a one-size-fits-all solution, iTiffin allowed customers to tailor their meal plans according to their dietary preferences and health goals. This flexibility ensured that customers received meals that aligned with their individual needs, which in turn helped to build trust and loyalty.

Customer feedback was an integral part of iTiffin's growth strategy. The company actively sought input from its users to continuously improve its service offerings. Customers were able to provide feedback on meal quality, portion sizes, and delivery timing, which helped the company fine-tune its operations. This approach to customer-centric service not only improved the overall user experience but also helped iTiffin build a positive reputation in the market.

The rapid growth of iTiffin can be attributed to the rising demand for health-focused meal delivery services, particularly in urban areas like Bangalore, where the startup first launched. The company's early success in attracting customers was fueled by a combination of effective digital marketing campaigns, word-of-mouth referrals, and partnerships with fitness centers and gyms. These marketing efforts helped to position iTiffin as a trusted provider of healthy meals, particularly among health-conscious consumers.

In the initial stages, iTiffin was able to scale its operations smoothly, thanks to its subscription model and focused customer base. The company's ability to maintain consistency in meal quality and delivery times contributed to its early growth. Customers who experienced positive interactions with the service were more likely to recommend it to others, creating a cycle of organic growth that helped the company expand its reach.

iTiffin's focus on customer retention was another key aspect of its early growth. The company offered incentives for customers to remain subscribed, such as discounts for long-term plans and loyalty rewards for regular customers. These initiatives helped iTiffin maintain a stable base of recurring revenue, which was crucial for sustaining its operations in the competitive food delivery market.

However, as iTiffin expanded to new cities and scaled up its operations, maintaining the same level of customer experience became more challenging. The company began facing logistical difficulties in managing deliveries across multiple locations, leading to inconsistencies in service. This decline in service quality would later contribute to customer churn and hamper iTiffin's ability to sustain its initial growth trajectory.

In summary, iTiffin's early growth was driven by its ability to deliver a personalized and convenient customer experience. By focusing on health and wellness, the company was able to attract a loyal customer base that valued its unique meal offerings. However, as the company expanded, it struggled to maintain the same level of service, which ultimately impacted its ability to retain customers.

5. Expansion and Scaling Challenges

iTiffin's early success in Bangalore prompted the company to explore expansion into other cities, including Mumbai and Delhi, two of India's largest urban markets. The founders believed that the demand for healthy, convenient meals was not just limited to Bangalore but was a growing trend across India. Encouraged by the positive response in their initial market, iTiffin sought to replicate its model in other metropolitan cities, hoping to tap into the vast population of working professionals, students, and fitness enthusiasts.

However, the rapid expansion introduced several operational challenges. Unlike Bangalore, where iTiffin had been able to establish close relationships with local vendors and chefs, new cities presented unfamiliar logistical hurdles. The supply chain, which had worked smoothly in a single city, became increasingly complicated as the company attempted to scale its operations across different geographic regions. Ensuring that meals were prepared and delivered on time in multiple cities required a more sophisticated logistical framework, one that iTiffin had not yet fully developed.

Additionally, scaling up meant that iTiffin had to forge new partnerships with restaurants and cloud kitchens in each city. While the company had carefully curated relationships with its partners in Bangalore, replicating these partnerships in other cities proved to be a daunting task. Different cities had different vendor capabilities, and not all partners could meet iTiffin's high standards for meal quality and consistency. As a result, the quality of meals began to vary from one city to another, which affected the overall customer experience and diluted the brand's reputation for providing healthy, reliable meals.

The rapid scaling also strained iTiffin's operational resources. Managing deliveries across multiple locations required a robust infrastructure and a well-coordinated delivery system, both of which were lacking as the company expanded. While iTiffin had optimized its operations for a single-city model, it was not prepared for the complexities of managing a larger, multi-city operation. This led to logistical bottlenecks, delays in meal deliveries, and increasing dissatisfaction among customers who had come to expect timely service.

Financial strain also became a significant challenge as iTiffin scaled. Expanding into new cities required substantial upfront investment in infrastructure, marketing, and hiring. The company had to spend heavily to build out its delivery networks, establish relationships with vendors, and promote its services in new markets. However, the return on these investments was slower than anticipated, as iTiffin struggled to gain the same traction in other cities as it had in Bangalore. The increased operational costs and slower-than-expected revenue growth began to take a toll on the company's financial health.

Moreover, the complexity of managing a growing workforce across multiple locations added to the challenges. iTiffin had to hire and train new staff in each city to manage logistics, handle customer service, and oversee operations. This stretched the company's resources thin, as it lacked the management bandwidth and experienced personnel needed to handle such rapid growth. The lack of experienced leadership in key areas such as logistics and operations exacerbated the company's growing pains.

In summary, iTiffin's expansion into new cities brought with it a host of challenges that the company was unprepared to handle. The complexities of scaling operations, managing new vendor relationships, and ensuring consistent service across multiple locations proved to be significant hurdles. These scaling challenges not only strained the company's resources but also contributed to a decline in service quality, which began to affect customer retention and the overall growth trajectory of the business.

6. Logistics Issues

As iTiffin expanded into multiple cities, the logistical challenges it faced became increasingly evident. One of the biggest issues was ensuring that meals were delivered fresh and on time, especially in cities where traffic congestion and infrastructure limitations made timely delivery a major obstacle. The promise of delivering healthy, freshly prepared meals to customers was central to iTiffin's value proposition, but as the company scaled, maintaining this promise became harder. Late deliveries became a recurring issue, frustrating customers who had subscribed to the service expecting reliable, timely meal deliveries.

Managing the supply chain for a food delivery service is inherently complex, and iTiffin's reliance on third-party vendors for meal preparation added another layer of difficulty. In its early stages, iTiffin had tight control over the quality of its meals because it worked with a select group of vendors in a single city. However, as the company expanded into new markets, it became increasingly challenging to ensure that vendors adhered to the same standards of quality and timeliness. This led to inconsistencies in meal quality, with some customers receiving meals that were undercooked, overcooked, or improperly portioned.

Furthermore, iTiffin's delivery network, which had been relatively small and manageable in Bangalore, struggled to scale efficiently across multiple cities. The company faced significant logistical bottlenecks as it attempted to coordinate deliveries across wider geographic areas with a growing number of customers. Unlike competitors who had invested heavily in building out their own logistics networks, iTiffin's delivery system relied heavily on third-party delivery services, which were often unreliable and difficult to manage. This led to frequent delays and incorrect orders, further eroding customer trust.

Another logistical challenge was maintaining the freshness and temperature of the meals during transit. Since iTiffin prided itself on delivering nutritious, freshly prepared meals, any delays in the delivery process compromised the quality of the food. Customers who received their meals late often found them to be cold or soggy, which diminished the appeal of the service. Maintaining temperature-controlled deliveries was an expensive proposition that iTiffin could not afford to implement effectively across all of its locations, especially given its financial constraints.

The lack of an efficient inventory management system further complicated logistics. As the number of orders increased, iTiffin struggled to manage its supply of ingredients and meal preparation schedules. This led to instances where certain meals were unavailable due to stock shortages, forcing the company to offer substitutions that were often not well-received by customers. The inconsistency in meal availability created dissatisfaction among customers who had subscribed to specific meal plans expecting consistent options.

The logistical issues were compounded by the company's rapid growth. In its rush to expand into new cities, iTiffin neglected to invest in the infrastructure needed to support its operations at scale. The company's systems and processes were not designed to handle the volume of orders that came with expansion, and this lack of scalability led to operational breakdowns. The result was a steady decline in the reliability of the service, which directly impacted customer satisfaction and loyalty.

In conclusion, iTiffin's logistical issues were a significant factor in its decline. The company's inability to manage its supply chain efficiently, coordinate reliable deliveries, and maintain meal quality at scale eroded customer trust and led to high levels of dissatisfaction. These challenges were exacerbated by iTiffin's rapid expansion, which outpaced its logistical capabilities and ultimately undermined its ability to deliver on its core value proposition of providing fresh, healthy, and convenient meals.

7. Customer Churn and Dissatisfaction

As logistical issues mounted, iTiffin began experiencing significant customer churn, with a growing number of users canceling their subscriptions due to dissatisfaction with the service. The promise of reliable, healthy meals delivered daily had attracted a loyal base of customers in the early stages, but as the company expanded and operational problems became more apparent, many customers began to lose confidence in the platform. Delays in delivery, inconsistent meal quality, and poor customer service were the primary reasons behind the increasing customer churn.

For a subscription-based business like iTiffin, customer retention is critical to long-term success. However, the platform's failure to address recurring issues such as late deliveries and incorrect orders resulted in a steady decline in user satisfaction. Customers who had initially subscribed for the convenience of regular, healthy meals found themselves frequently dealing with service disruptions, which diminished the value of the subscription. Many customers expressed frustration over the declining quality of the service, particularly as iTiffin expanded into new cities without adequately resolving its operational challenges.

Moreover, as competitors like Swiggy and Zomato continued to improve their logistics and expand their meal options, iTiffin struggled to retain customers who were drawn to the larger platforms' more reliable service and greater variety. The lack of differentiation between iTiffin and its larger, better-funded competitors became increasingly apparent, particularly as customers became more demanding and the market more competitive. While iTiffin initially carved out a niche for itself by focusing on health-conscious consumers, its inability to consistently deliver on its promises caused many users to switch to more established platforms.

Customer complaints began to pile up, and iTiffin's ability to respond effectively to these complaints was limited. The company's customer service infrastructure was not equipped to handle the volume of issues arising from its expanding operations. Customers who encountered problems with their orders often struggled to get timely resolutions, further compounding their frustration. The lack of a responsive customer support team only served to accelerate the churn, as customers who felt ignored or neglected chose to take their business elsewhere.

In addition to logistical issues, meal quality began to decline as iTiffin scaled. Many customers reported that the meals they received were inconsistent in taste, portion size, and freshness. This decline in meal quality was a direct result of the company's strained relationships with its vendor partners, who were struggling to keep up with the increasing demand. As meal quality became less predictable, more customers canceled their subscriptions, citing dissatisfaction with the food.

To make matters worse, iTiffin's attempts to address customer churn through promotions and discounts were largely ineffective. While these offers initially helped to slow the rate of cancellations, they did little to resolve the underlying issues that were causing customers to leave in the first place. As a result, the company found itself in a vicious cycle: offering discounts to retain customers while simultaneously grappling with rising operational costs and diminishing service quality.

In conclusion, customer churn became one of the key challenges that contributed to iTiffin's downfall. The company's inability to resolve its logistical issues, maintain meal quality, and provide effective customer support led to a steady decline in user satisfaction. As customers left the platform in increasing numbers, iTiffin struggled to recover, and its efforts to retain users through promotions and discounts failed to address the root causes of dissatisfaction.

8. Market Competition

As iTiffin grappled with its internal operational challenges, the external pressures from an increasingly competitive food delivery market intensified. The company faced significant competition from larger, more established players like Swiggy, Zomato, and FreshMenu, which were not only well-funded but also rapidly expanding their service offerings. These competitors had already built out strong logistical networks and were offering a wider range of meal options, which made it difficult for iTiffin to maintain its unique selling proposition as a health-focused, subscription-based meal delivery service.

Swiggy and Zomato, in particular, posed a serious threat to iTiffin's growth and sustainability. These platforms had the financial resources to invest heavily in marketing, logistics, and technology, which allowed them to offer faster deliveries and a broader selection of meals. Unlike iTiffin, which was limited to offering a narrow range of curated, nutritionist-approved meals, Swiggy and Zomato gave customers access to a wide variety of restaurant options, from fast food to gourmet cuisine. This variety appealed to customers who wanted more flexibility in their meal choices, and many of iTiffin's subscribers began to shift their loyalty to these larger platforms.

In addition to meal variety, Swiggy and Zomato also offered more reliable delivery services. Both platforms had invested heavily in building their own delivery fleets, which allowed them to control the logistics of meal delivery more efficiently. This resulted in faster, more consistent deliveries compared to iTiffin, which relied heavily on third-party delivery services that often failed to meet customer expectations. As a result, iTiffin found itself at a significant disadvantage in terms of delivery speed and reliability, which were critical factors in retaining customers in the competitive food delivery market.

Another key area where iTiffin struggled to compete was in pricing and promotions. Larger platforms like Swiggy and Zomato had the financial backing to offer regular discounts, promotions, and loyalty programs to attract and retain customers. These promotions were particularly appealing to price-sensitive consumers, many of whom began to switch from iTiffin to platforms that offered better deals. iTiffin, with its limited financial resources, was unable to compete with these aggressive marketing strategies. While the company did offer occasional discounts, they were not frequent or significant enough to stem the tide of customer churn.

FreshMenu, another competitor, posed a unique challenge to iTiffin by offering a curated menu similar to iTiffin's but with a wider variety of options. FreshMenu capitalized on the growing demand for gourmet meals delivered to homes and offices, and its ability to rotate its menu daily while maintaining high food quality made it a formidable competitor. FreshMenu's focus on gourmet-style food also attracted a segment of the health-conscious market that iTiffin had initially targeted. This overlap in target audiences further eroded iTiffin's customer base, as users found FreshMenu's offerings to be more diverse and appealing.

Moreover, as these competitors scaled rapidly, they were able to forge stronger relationships with restaurant partners, allowing them to expand their menus and maintain high service standards. iTiffin, on the other hand, faced difficulties in managing its partnerships with vendors as it expanded, which affected both meal quality and delivery times. As copetitors continued to improve their service offerings, iTiffin's operational struggles became more apparent, and the platform struggled to maintain its relevance in the crowded market.

In summary, iTiffin's inability to compete effectively with larger, more resourceful competitors like Swiggy, Zomato, and FreshMenu played a significant role in its downfall. The broader meal variety, faster deliveries, and aggressive promotions offered by these platforms attracted customers away from iTiffin, which lacked the financial and logistical capabilities to keep up. As a result, iTiffin's market position weakened, and it struggled to retain its customer base in the face of stiff competition.

9. Financial Strain

The combination of logistical inefficiencies, customer churn, and rising competition placed immense financial strain on iTiffin. While the company had enjoyed early success with a steady stream of subscriptions, the costs associated with expanding into new cities, managing partnerships, and maintaining quality control quickly outpaced its revenue. The subscription model, which had initially seemed like a reliable source of recurring income, began to show cracks as the company struggled to retain its customers amid growing dissatisfaction and competition.

One of the primary financial challenges iTiffin faced was the increasing cost of logistics. As the company expanded its operations to multiple cities, the complexity of managing deliveries grew exponentially. The reliance on third-party delivery services, combined with inefficient routing and delivery delays, led to higher operational costs that the company had not anticipated. These costs included not only the expense of deliveries but also the resources required to manage customer complaints, issue refunds, and address service disruptions. This financial drain made it difficult for iTiffin to invest in improving its operations or scaling its delivery infrastructure.

Additionally, as iTiffin expanded its service to new markets, the company had to invest heavily in marketing and customer acquisition efforts. Competing against well-established platforms like Swiggy and Zomato required substantial marketing expenditure, which further strained iTiffin's financial resources. Unlike its competitors, who had raised significant venture capital funding, iTiffin had a more modest financial backing, limiting its ability to scale its marketing efforts effectively. As a result, the company found it increasingly difficult to attract new customers and maintain a steady flow of subscriptions.

The rising costs of maintaining vendor relationships also contributed to iTiffin's financial strain. As the company expanded, it had to negotiate new contracts with vendors in different cities, many of whom demanded higher payments due to the increased scale of operations. The cost of sourcing fresh, high-quality ingredients also escalated, particularly as iTiffin struggled to ensure consistency across its meal plans. The financial burden of managing these relationships, combined with the need to ensure timely payments to vendors, placed additional pressure on iTiffin's already limited resources.

iTiffin's financial struggles were compounded by its inability to secure additional funding. While the company had raised initial seed capital to launch its operations, it found it difficult to attract new investors as its financial performance declined. Potential investors were wary of the company's high operational costs, inconsistent customer retention, and the growing dominance of competitors in the market. Without fresh capital, iTiffin was unable to invest in improving its logistics, expanding its product offerings, or enhancing its marketing efforts, all of which were necessary to remain competitive in the fast-growing food delivery space.

As revenue growth slowed and costs continued to rise, iTiffin's cash flow problems became more acute. The company was unable to achieve the economies of scale needed to offset its rising operational expenses, leading to a vicious cycle of financial instability. The lack of profitability, combined with mounting debts and unpaid vendor invoices, eventually forced iTiffin to scale back its operations. Despite efforts to cut costs and streamline operations, the company's financial health continued to deteriorate.

In conclusion, iTiffin's financial strain was a major factor in its downfall. The rising costs of logistics, marketing, and vendor management, combined with its inability to secure additional funding, left the company unable to compete effectively in the market. The financial pressure ultimately led to a decline in service quality and customer satisfaction, which further exacerbated the company's financial woes and contributed to its eventual collapse.

10. Attempts to Pivot

As iTiffin's financial struggles worsened, the company attempted to pivot its business model in a last-ditch effort to turn the business around. One of the key pivots iTiffin explored was expanding its menu to include a wider range of meal options, hoping that this would attract a broader audience and provide the variety that customers were increasingly demanding. The goal was to diversify beyond the strict health-focused meal plans that had initially defined iTiffin, offering meals that catered to a wider range of tastes and preferences, while still maintaining a focus on balanced nutrition.

However, this shift in strategy came with its own set of challenges. Expanding the menu meant that iTiffin had to forge new partnerships with additional vendors, many of whom did not have the same level of experience or commitment to health-focused meals. This made it difficult for the company to maintain the same standards of quality and consistency that had initially attracted its customer base. While the expanded menu did offer more variety, it diluted iTiffin's brand identity, leaving customers unsure of what the platform truly stood for.In addition to expanding its menu, iTiffin also explored the possibility of entering the corporate catering market, targeting companies that wanted to offer healthy meal options to their employees. This pivot was seen as a way to diversify the company's revenue streams and reduce its reliance on individual consumer subscriptions. The corporate catering model offered the potential for larger, more predictable orders, which could help stabilize iTiffin's cash flow and reduce its logistical complexity by delivering bulk orders to office locations rather than individual households.

Despite the potential of the corporate catering market, iTiffin struggled to execute this pivot effectively. The company lacked the resources and infrastructure needed to manage large-scale corporate orders, and its operational inefficiencies persisted even in this new business model. Furthermore, iTiffin's reputation had already begun to suffer due to its declining service quality, making it difficult to secure corporate clients who were willing to trust the company with their meal services. As a result, the corporate catering pivot failed to gain traction, leaving iTiffin still reliant on its struggling subscription model.

Another pivot iTiffin attempted was the introduction of meal kits, allowing customers to prepare their own healthy meals at home using pre-portioned ingredients provided by the company. This pivot aimed to tap into the growing trend of meal kits, which were becoming popular in urban areas as a way for busy professionals to cook healthy meals without the hassle of grocery shopping. However, iTiffin's meal kit offering failed to stand out in a market already dominated by established players like FreshMenu and other meal kit services, and the logistics of delivering fresh ingredients only added to the company's existing operational challenges.

Ultimately, iTiffin's attempts to pivot came too late and were not executed with the strategic focus required to turn the company around. The pivots were reactive rather than proactive, driven by the company's desperation to find new sources of revenue rather than a well-thought-out plan for growth. Each pivot introduced new operational complexities that the company was ill-equipped to handle, and none of the pivots addressed the underlying issues of logistical inefficiency and customer dissatisfaction that had plagued iTiffin from the start.

In conclusion, iTiffin's attempts to pivot its business model were unsuccessful in reversing the company's fortunes. The expanded menu, corporate catering, and meal kit offerings all failed to gain the traction needed to offset the company's financial losses and operational struggles. The pivots were too little, too late, and iTiffin's inability to execute them effectively only hastened its decline. These failed pivots ultimately highlighted the company's deeper issues, which could not be solved by simply expanding its product offerings.

Key Points

- **iTiffin's journey** illustrates the complexities of scaling a niche business in the competitive meal delivery market, particularly one focused on health-conscious consumers.
- **Logistical challenges** and inefficiencies in managing meal preparation, delivery, and customer service led to operational strains, which affected iTiffin's ability to meet growing demand.
- **High customer churn** was a major issue for iTiffin, as the company struggled to retain its user base due to inconsistent service quality and delivery delays, despite its unique health-focused offerings.

- **Limited funding and cash flow problems** hindered iTiffin's ability to scale effectively, leaving the company vulnerable to competition from larger, better-funded food delivery platforms.
- **iTiffin's failure** highlights the importance of balancing niche market focus with operational scalability, while also maintaining consistent service quality to retain a loyal customer base.

Satyam Tripathi

Chapter 8. Fynd: Bridging the Online and Offline Divide, Yet Falling Short

1. Introduction to Fynd

Fynd, founded in 2013, emerged as a unique player in the Indian e-commerce ecosystem with its innovative online-to-offline (O2O) retail platform. The company's primary goal was to merge the benefits of both online shopping and offline retail by allowing customers to discover and purchase fashion products from nearby physical stores. The O2O model was designed to provide a seamless shopping experience by giving users the convenience of online shopping while leveraging the real-time inventory of local stores. This was particularly appealing to customers who wanted faster deliveries and the assurance that the products they were ordering were immediately available in their vicinity.

The idea behind Fynd was to solve the challenges faced by both customers and retailers in the traditional e-commerce and brick-and-mortar setups. For customers, the frustration of discovering that a desired product was out of stock or faced delayed shipping was a common issue. By offering real-time inventory updates, Fynd allowed customers to check product availability at nearby stores, ensuring that items could be delivered quickly or even picked up in-store. For local retailers, Fynd provided an opportunity to reach a wider online audience without the need for significant investment in digital infrastructure. By connecting retailers to online shoppers, Fynd offered an additional sales channel that helped boost foot traffic and sales in physical stores.

The founding team at Fynd, which included Harsh Shah, Farooq Adam, and Sreeraman MG, brought diverse experience from technology and retail sectors, allowing them to build a platform that combined technological innovation with deep retail insights. Their goal was to create a system that would integrate local retail inventories with an online platform in real time, offering a streamlined shopping experience for users and solving inefficiencies in the supply chain for retailers. The vision was ambitious, as it required real-time synchronization between offline stores and the online platform, along with logistical coordination for prompt deliveries.

Fynd's focus on fashion retail, a rapidly growing sector in India, positioned the company to capitalize on the increasing demand for convenience and fast access to trendy products. The platform's initial launch was well-received, particularly in urban areas where customers were used to shopping online but often experienced delays due to centralized warehouses. Fynd aimed to leverage the network of physical stores in these areas to speed up deliveries, offering same-day or even quicker delivery options that traditional e-commerce platforms struggled to match.

The platform's user-friendly app and website allowed customers to search for specific fashion items across a range of stores, check availability in real-time, and place orders for quick delivery. By focusing on local inventory, Fynd sought to eliminate the long waiting times associated with conventional e-commerce models, where products often had to be shipped from centralized warehouses located far from the customer's location. Fynd's innovation lay in its ability to offer a seamless blend of online and offline shopping, appealing to customers who wanted the best of both worlds.

In the early stages, Fynd's approach resonated with a niche segment of tech-savvy, fashion-conscious urban consumers who were looking for convenience and immediacy in their shopping experiences. The platform's emphasis on connecting customers with local stores also supported the growing trend of hyper-local commerce, where consumers preferred buying products from nearby locations to reduce delivery times. Fynd’s ability to tap into this trend helped the company gain traction in its initial market, particularly among young professionals and urban shoppers who valued time-saving solutions.

However, despite the initial promise and innovation of Fynd's business model, the company faced significant challenges as it began to scale. Integrating real-time inventory systems with multiple offline stores across different locations proved to be more complex than anticipated. Additionally, the platform’s ability to compete with established e-commerce giants like Amazon and Flipkart, which offered vast product catalogs and extensive delivery networks, was an uphill battle. These challenges, along with financial struggles, would later contribute to the platform’s decline.

In conclusion, Fynd’s innovative approach to bridging the gap between online and offline shopping through real-time inventory updates offered a unique proposition in the Indian e-commerce market. By focusing on fashion retail and leveraging local stores for quick deliveries, Fynd initially gained traction among urban consumers looking for a convenient shopping experience. However, the complexities of scaling this model and the intense competition from larger players in the space presented significant challenges that would eventually impact the company's sustainability.

2. Business Model and Unique Proposition

Fynd's business model was designed to bridge the gap between online shopping and offline retail by offering an integrated platform that connected local stores with online customers. The key to this model was real-time inventory management, which allowed customers to browse products available at physical retail stores near them. Unlike traditional e-commerce platforms that relied on centralized warehouses, Fynd tapped into the existing inventory of local stores, providing a more decentralized approach to product delivery. This allowed customers to shop online with the added assurance that the products they were purchasing were available in a nearby store, leading to faster deliveries and fewer stock issues.

The company's unique proposition lay in its ability to combine the best aspects of both online and offline shopping experiences. For customers, Fynd offered the convenience of browsing and purchasing products online while ensuring faster delivery times by using local store inventories. This eliminated the long delivery windows typically associated with e-commerce platforms that shipped products from distant warehouses. For retailers, Fynd provided a digital storefront, allowing them to reach a broader audience without the need for significant investment in building or maintaining an online presence. This partnership enabled local retailers to compete in the growing e-commerce space without overhauling their traditional business models.

One of Fynd's key differentiators was its ability to provide real-time inventory updates. This ensured that customers could see accurate product availability before placing an order, reducing the likelihood of purchasing an item that was out of stock. This feature was particularly useful in the fashion retail space, where inventory turnover can be high, and customers often want the latest trends. By syncing online listings with in-store inventories, Fynd allowed customers to reserve or purchase items that were guaranteed to be available for immediate delivery or in-store pickup.

Fynd's O2O model also provided customers with the flexibility to choose between home delivery and in-store pickup. This added layer of convenience appealed to users who preferred to avoid delivery fees or wanted to try on items before making a final purchase. The option of picking up products from a nearby store also gave Fynd a competitive edge in terms of delivery speed, as customers could access their purchases immediately without waiting for them to be shipped. This blend of online browsing and offline fulfillment was central to Fynd's appeal.

Another aspect of Fynd's business model was its ability to support retailers in managing their digital presence. Many local stores lacked the technological expertise or financial resources to create an effective e-commerce platform, which limited their ability to compete with larger retail chains and online-only stores. Fynd offered these retailers an all-in-one solution, providing them with the tools to manage their inventory, update product listings, and handle orders through a single platform. This not only streamlined operations for retailers but also gave them access to a wider, tech-savvy customer base that they might not have reached otherwise.

In addition to benefiting retailers, Fynd's business model also focused on providing a better customer experience. The platform's ability to connect customers to local stores and offer same-day or next-day delivery differentiated it from larger e-commerce players that typically required longer shipping times. This hyper-local approach to fulfillment appealed to customers who valued immediacy and convenience in their shopping experience, especially in urban areas where delivery speed is often a deciding factor.

However, despite these advantages, Fynd's business model also had inherent challenges. Integrating inventory management systems across multiple independent retailers required significant coordination and technological investment. Maintaining real-time updates was critical to the platform’s success, but it proved to be a complex task as the company scaled. Additionally, Fynd's reliance on local retailers for fulfillment meant that the platform was heavily dependent on the operational efficiency of these stores, which varied widely in terms of stock management and delivery capabilities.

In summary, Fynd’s business model offered a unique proposition in the e-commerce landscape by combining online convenience with offline fulfillment through real-time inventory updates. The platform's ability to provide faster deliveries by leveraging local store inventories and its support for retailers looking to expand their digital presence were key differentiators. However, the complexity of integrating multiple retail systems and the reliance on external partners for fulfillment presented ongoing challenges for the company.

3. Early Market Success

Fynd’s initial foray into the Indian retail market was marked by early success, particularly in urban areas where customers were already familiar with online shopping but often experienced frustration with delayed deliveries or out-of-stock items. The platform’s ability to offer real-time inventory updates and faster delivery times resonated with a tech-savvy, urban consumer base that valued convenience and immediacy. Fynd quickly gained traction by positioning itself as an innovative alternative to traditional e-commerce platforms, offering users the best of both online and offline shopping experiences.

The platform’s early success was also driven by its strategic partnerships with local fashion retailers. By onboarding stores with high customer footfall and popular fashion brands, Fynd was able to offer a curated selection of trendy products that appealed to its target audience. The platform's fashion focus differentiated it from other e-commerce giants that catered to a wider variety of categories, allowing Fynd to carve out a niche in the highly competitive fashion retail space. Additionally, the platform's user-friendly interface, which made it easy for customers to browse products, check availability, and place orders, contributed to its growing popularity.

One of the key factors that contributed to Fynd's early success was its focus on providing a seamless, hyper-local shopping experience. Unlike other e-commerce platforms that shipped products from centralized warehouses, Fynd leveraged local store inventories to fulfill orders, significantly reducing delivery times. In cities like Mumbai, Bangalore, and Delhi, where traffic congestion often caused delays in traditional delivery models, Fynd's ability to offer same-day or next-day delivery gave it a competitive advantage. This focus on speed and convenience appealed to urban consumers who were accustomed to the immediate gratification of offline shopping.

Fynd's initial marketing campaigns also played a crucial role in attracting users to the platform. The company positioned itself as a cutting-edge solution for fashion-conscious individuals who wanted the latest trends without the hassle of waiting for deliveries. By targeting young professionals and urban dwellers who were early adopters of technology, Fynd was able to generate significant interest in its platform. Word-of-mouth and digital marketing campaigns on social media further amplified Fynd's reach, helping the platform build a loyal user base in its early stages.

Moreover, Fynd's customer-centric approach contributed to its initial success. The platform offered multiple payment options, including cash on delivery, credit/debit cards, and mobile wallets, catering to the diverse preferences of Indian consumers. Fynd also implemented a hassle-free return policy, which gave customers confidence in making purchases, knowing that they could easily return items if they were not satisfied. This focus on convenience and customer satisfaction helped build trust in the platform, leading to repeat purchases and increased customer loyalty.

Fynd's early growth was not limited to consumers; the platform also attracted interest from retailers who saw the potential of reaching a wider audience through Fynd's digital platform. For smaller retailers, Fynd provided an opportunity to tap into the growing e-commerce market without investing heavily in their own digital infrastructure. This symbiotic relationship between Fynd and local retailers helped the company scale its operations quickly, adding more stores to its platform and expanding its product offerings.

However, as Fynd expanded, the company began to encounter operational challenges that threatened to undermine its early success. Managing real-time inventory updates across multiple stores in different locations proved to be more difficult as the number of retailers on the platform grew. While Fynd's model worked well in a controlled environment with a limited number of stores, scaling this model presented significant logistical and technological hurdles.

In conclusion, Fynd's early market success was fueled by its innovative approach to online shopping, which combined the convenience of e-commerce with the immediacy of offline retail. The platform's ability to offer real-time inventory updates, faster deliveries, and a curated selection of fashion products resonated with urban consumers who valued convenience and speed. However, as the company scaled, the operational complexities of managing multiple retail partners and maintaining real-time updates began to surface, presenting challenges to Fynd's growth trajectory.

4. Expansion and Partnerships

Fynd's early success in major urban centers led the company to pursue rapid expansion, both in terms of geographic reach and the range of products available on its platform. The company's goal was to scale its O2O model to more cities across India, while also expanding its partnerships with both local and national retail brands. To achieve this, Fynd focused on building partnerships with well-known fashion retailers, allowing the platform to offer a broader selection of products and attract a wider audience.

As part of its expansion strategy, Fynd began partnering with larger retail chains, such as Reliance Trends, Central, and Brand Factory, to increase the diversity of products on its platform. These partnerships not only helped Fynd expand its product catalog but also enhanced its brand credibility, as customers were able to shop for popular, trusted brands through the platform. By collaborating with established retail chains, Fynd was able to appeal to a broader customer base that was already familiar with these brands but wanted the convenience of shopping online.

Fynd's expansion also involved integrating new features into its platform to enhance the user experience. One of the key features introduced was same-day delivery in select cities, which aimed to provide customers with an even faster and more convenient shopping experience. This feature was particularly popular in metropolitan areas where customers were accustomed to the immediacy of offline shopping but appreciated the convenience of browsing products online. Fynd's ability to deliver products within a few hours of placing an order set it apart from larger e-commerce platforms, which typically required several days for delivery.

Another aspect of Fynd's expansion was its focus on mobile commerce. As smartphone penetration increased across India, Fynd capitalized on the growing trend of mobile shopping by optimizing its platform for mobile devices. The Fynd app became the primary touchpoint for customers, offering a seamless shopping experience with features like push notifications for new arrivals, personalized recommendations, and easy checkout options. The app's intuitive design and user-friendly interface contributed to Fynd's growing customer base, particularly among younger, tech-savvy consumers.

In addition to geographic and product expansion, Fynd also explored opportunities to enter new categories beyond fashion. The company began experimenting with adding accessories, footwear, and lifestyle products to its platform in an effort to diversify its offerings and increase its average order value. While fashion remained the core focus of the platform, these new categories allowed Fynd to capture a larger share of the online retail market and attract customers looking for a more comprehensive shopping experience.

However, as Fynd expanded, the complexities of managing a growing number of partnerships and ensuring real-time inventory updates became more apparent. The platform's success depended heavily on its ability to provide accurate, up-to-the-minute inventory information, but as the number of stores and products on the platform increased, maintaining this level of accuracy became a challenge. Retail partners were responsible for updating their inventory in real-time, but many lacked the technological infrastructure or processes to do so efficiently. This led to frequent discrepancies between online listings and actual stock levels, resulting in customer dissatisfaction.

The expansion also strained Fynd's logistics network. As the platform grew, coordinating deliveries from multiple stores across different cities became more difficult. Ensuring that products were delivered on time and in good condition required significant investment in logistics infrastructure, which Fynd struggled to scale effectively. Inconsistent delivery times and logistical bottlenecks began to affect the customer experience, particularly in cities where Fynd had recently expanded.

In summary, Fynd's expansion and partnerships played a crucial role in the company's growth, helping it scale its operations and broaden its product offerings. Partnerships with larger retail chains and the introduction of new features like same-day delivery helped Fynd attract a wider audience and enhance the customer experience. However, the complexities of managing a growing number of partnerships and scaling logistics posed significant challenges that would later impact the platform's ability to maintain its early success.

5. Inventory Management Challenges

As Fynd expanded its operations and onboarded more retailers, the complexity of managing real-time inventory across multiple stores became one of the platform's biggest challenges. The platform's business model relied heavily on its ability to provide accurate, up-to-date inventory information to customers, ensuring that the products they saw online were available for immediate purchase and delivery. However, as Fynd scaled, maintaining this level of accuracy across a growing network of retailers proved to be a significant hurdle.

One of the primary issues Fynd faced was the inconsistency in how retailers managed their inventories. Many of the local stores that partnered with Fynd lacked the technological infrastructure to update their stock levels in real time. This led to frequent discrepancies between the products listed as available on Fynd's platform and the actual stock levels in the stores. Customers would often place orders for items that appeared to be in stock, only to be informed later that the product was unavailable. These stock mismatches resulted in frustration for customers and damaged Fynd's reputation as a reliable platform.

The challenges of real-time inventory management were further exacerbated by the fact that Fynd worked with a diverse range of retailers, each with its own inventory management systems and processes. Some stores used outdated or manual methods for tracking stock, while others lacked the staff or technology to update inventory in real-time. As a result, Fynd struggled to ensure consistency across its platform, leading to a fragmented and unreliable shopping experience for customers.

To address these issues, Fynd invested in developing its own inventory management system, which it encouraged retailers to adopt. This system aimed to streamline the process of updating stock levels and integrating them with the platform in real time. However, many smaller retailers were resistant to adopting new technology, either due to cost concerns or a lack of technical expertise. This resistance hindered Fynd's efforts to create a seamless inventory management system, further complicating the platform's operations as it scaled.

Another challenge was managing the inventory of popular items. Fashion retail is a fast-moving industry, with trends changing rapidly and certain items selling out quickly. Fynd's inability to provide real-time inventory updates for these high-demand products meant that customers were often left disappointed when the items they wanted were no longer available. This problem was particularly acute during sales or promotional periods, when demand spiked and retailers struggled to keep up with stock updates.

In addition to managing inventory discrepancies, Fynd also faced challenges in forecasting demand and ensuring that retailers were adequately stocked with popular items. The platform lacked the sophisticated demand forecasting tools used by larger e-commerce players, which made it difficult to predict which products would sell quickly and which would remain on shelves. As a result, Fynd often found itself in a position where popular items were out of stock, while less popular products remained available, leading to inefficiencies in inventory management.

The lack of reliable inventory data also affected Fynd's ability to offer same-day or next-day delivery, one of the platform's key selling points. If an item listed as available turned out to be out of stock, the delivery process would be delayed as Fynd had to cancel the order or source the product from a different store. These delays undermined the platform's promise of fast, convenient deliveries and contributed to customer dissatisfaction.

In conclusion, inventory management was one of the most significant challenges Fynd faced as it scaled. The platform's reliance on real-time inventory updates from a diverse network of retailers led to frequent stock mismatches, causing frustration for customers and damaging the platform's credibility. Despite efforts to streamline inventory management through technology, Fynd struggled to maintain consistency across its network of stores, which ultimately affected the overall customer experience and contributed to the platform's operational difficulties.

6. Funding Struggles

Fynd's innovative business model and early success attracted some initial funding, but as the company sought to scale, securing additional rounds of investment became increasingly difficult. While Fynd had a unique proposition in the O2O space, investors were hesitant to commit large amounts of capital due to the inherent challenges of managing real-time inventory across multiple offline stores. The complexities of integrating disparate retail systems, coupled with the logistical hurdles of delivering products from local stores, made investors question the scalability and profitability of Fynd's business model.

One of the primary reasons for Fynd's funding struggles was the intense competition in the e-commerce sector. Larger players like Amazon, Flipkart, and Myntra dominated the online retail space, and these companies had already secured significant funding to build out their logistics networks, technology infrastructure, and marketing campaigns. Compared to these giants, Fynd's business model seemed niche and less scalable, particularly as the company faced operational challenges related to inventory management and delivery logistics. Investors were concerned that Fynd would struggle to compete with these well-funded competitors, limiting the platform's growth potential.

Fynd's reliance on external retailers for fulfillment also raised concerns among investors. Unlike traditional e-commerce platforms that controlled their own supply chains and warehouses, Fynd was dependent on its retail partners to manage inventory and deliveries. This lack of control over key aspects of the business made it difficult for Fynd to ensure consistency and reliability, which in turn made investors wary of the platform's ability to scale effectively. The fragmented nature of the retail partnerships added a layer of complexity that made Fynd a riskier investment compared to other e-commerce platforms.

Another factor contributing to Fynd's funding struggles was the platform's inability to demonstrate a clear path to profitability. While Fynd had seen early success in urban areas, the costs associated with managing real-time inventory, coordinating deliveries, and maintaining a large network of retail partners were high. The platform's operational expenses continued to rise as it expanded, but its revenue growth was slower than anticipated due to the challenges of scaling its business model. Investors were hesitant to pour more money into a platform that had not yet proven its ability to achieve profitability at scale.

To mitigate these concerns, Fynd explored various strategies to attract new funding, including diversifying its product offerings and expanding into new categories such as footwear and accessories. The company also sought to improve its technology infrastructure by developing its own inventory management system, which it hoped would streamline operations and reduce costs. However, these efforts were not enough to convince investors that Fynd could overcome its operational challenges and compete with larger e-commerce players.

The lack of consistent funding forced Fynd to operate with limited resources, which further exacerbated its operational issues. The company struggled to invest in the technology and logistics infrastructure needed to scale its platform and improve the customer experience. Without the necessary capital to support its growth, Fynd found it difficult to expand its operations, onboard new retailers, and reach new markets, all of which were critical to sustaining its business model.

In conclusion, Fynd's funding struggles were a major obstacle to the company's growth and sustainability. While the platform's unique O2O model initially attracted interest from investors, the operational complexities of managing real-time inventory and the competitive landscape made it difficult for Fynd to secure the funding needed to scale effectively. The lack of consistent investment limited Fynd's ability to improve its technology, expand its operations, and compete with larger players in the market, ultimately contributing to the company's decline.

7. Competition in the E-commerce Space

Fynd operated in an e-commerce landscape that was already dominated by massive players such as Amazon, Flipkart, and Myntra. These companies had built extensive product catalogs, advanced logistics networks, and aggressive pricing strategies that made it difficult for smaller platforms like Fynd to compete. While Fynd offered a unique O2O (online-to-offline) business model that catered to fashion retail, the sheer scale and resources of its competitors presented a significant challenge to the company's growth and sustainability.

Amazon and Flipkart, in particular, were formidable competitors due to their deep pockets and established presence in the Indian e-commerce market. Both companies had already invested heavily in logistics infrastructure, allowing them to offer faster deliveries, even to smaller towns and rural areas. In contrast, Fynd's reliance on local retailers for fulfillment limited its ability to match the delivery speed and geographical reach of these e-commerce giants. As a result, Fynd struggled to attract customers who valued convenience and speed, especially in cities where same-day or next-day delivery had become the norm.

Another competitive pressure came from Myntra, which, like Fynd, specialized in fashion retail. Myntra, backed by Flipkart, had a much larger product catalog, offering everything from high-street fashion to premium brands. Myntra's extensive network of partnerships with global and local fashion brands gave it a significant edge over Fynd, whose partnerships were more limited to local retailers. Moreover, Myntra's highly developed logistics capabilities allowed it to offer a seamless shopping experience, from browsing to fast delivery, which Fynd found difficult to replicate at scale.

Pricing was another area where Fynd faced stiff competition. Larger platforms like Amazon, Flipkart, and Myntra could afford to offer deep discounts, promotional deals, and loyalty programs to attract price-sensitive customers. These promotions helped retain existing customers while drawing new ones into their ecosystem. Fynd, on the other hand, operated on thinner margins due to its reliance on external retail partners and the complexities of managing real-time inventory. The platform could not match the aggressive pricing strategies of its competitors, which made it less attractive to customers looking for the best deals.

Additionally, Fynd's limited product catalog made it difficult for the platform to compete with the variety offered by larger players. While Fynd focused on fashion, the likes of Amazon and Flipkart provided a one-stop-shop experience, offering products across multiple categories, from electronics and home goods to groceries and fashion. This vast selection made it more convenient for customers to consolidate their purchases on a single platform, reducing the likelihood that they would turn to Fynd for their fashion needs alone. The broader appeal of Amazon and Flipkart's extensive product offerings was a significant advantage that Fynd struggled to counteract.

Another competitive disadvantage for Fynd was the level of investment that its rivals were making in technology. Amazon, Flipkart, and Myntra had the resources to develop advanced recommendation algorithms, personalized marketing, and AI-driven customer support systems, all of which enhanced the customer experience. Fynd, with its limited funding, was unable to make similar investments in technology, which made it harder to keep up with the personalized and seamless experiences provided by these larger platforms. Customers increasingly expected these sophisticated features as part of their online shopping experience, and Fynd's inability to offer them became a major drawback.

Furthermore, the larger players were expanding their logistics capabilities to include in-house delivery systems, allowing them to control the entire supply chain from warehouse to doorstep. This control over logistics gave them a significant advantage in terms of efficiency and reliability, while Fynd, which relied on the delivery capabilities of its retail partners, struggled to maintain consistent delivery standards. Delays, missed deliveries, and inventory discrepancies became frequent complaints among Fynd customers, further eroding its competitiveness.

In conclusion, Fynd operated in a highly competitive e-commerce market dominated by giants like Amazon, Flipkart, and Myntra. These platforms had superior logistics, pricing strategies, and product variety, which made it difficult for Fynd to attract and retain customers. While Fynd's O2O model offered a unique proposition, it lacked the resources and scale to compete effectively with its larger rivals. The intense competition in the market played a significant role in Fynd's inability to maintain its early growth and ultimately contributed to its challenges in sustaining the business.

8. Logistics and Delivery Issues

As Fynd scaled its operations, logistics and delivery issues became a recurring challenge that significantly impacted the platform's ability to meet customer expectations. Unlike larger e-commerce platforms like Amazon and Flipkart, which had their own delivery networks and warehouses, Fynd relied on its retail partners to manage both inventory and delivery. This decentralized approach introduced a range of logistical complexities, making it difficult for the platform to offer consistent and timely deliveries, particularly as it expanded into new cities.

One of the main logistical challenges for Fynd was coordinating deliveries from multiple offline stores across different locations. Each store had its own delivery capabilities, and there was little standardization in terms of how deliveries were handled. Some stores were able to fulfill orders quickly, while others struggled with delays due to inadequate delivery infrastructure or staffing shortages. This lack of uniformity in delivery times created an inconsistent experience for customers, who often received their orders later than expected or in multiple shipments from different stores.

Fynd's promise of offering same-day or next-day delivery in select cities was a key selling point for the platform, but as the company expanded, it became increasingly difficult to fulfill this promise. The platform relied on its retail partners to dispatch products to customers, but many of these stores did not have the necessary logistics infrastructure to support fast delivery. Delays in processing orders, incorrect stock availability, and miscommunications between the stores and the platform further compounded the issue, leading to frustrated customers who had expected a seamless shopping experience.

Another logistical challenge was the management of last-mile delivery, which is the final leg of the delivery process from the store to the customer's location. Fynd's reliance on third-party delivery services introduced additional complexity, as the platform had little control over the quality and reliability of these services. In many cases, customers reported receiving damaged or incomplete orders, or they experienced long delays in delivery due to issues with third-party logistics providers. These delivery failures hurt Fynd's reputation, particularly in comparison to larger e-commerce platforms that had more robust, in-house delivery networks.

Inventory mismatches also created logistical bottlenecks. As mentioned earlier, Fynd's ability to provide real-time inventory updates was critical to its success. However, when customers placed orders for items that were marked as available but were actually out of stock in the store, the delivery process would be delayed or canceled entirely. This created confusion for both customers and delivery partners, as orders had to be adjusted or rerouted, leading to longer wait times and increased operational costs for Fynd.

In an effort to mitigate these issues, Fynd attempted to streamline its logistics by introducing centralized control over certain aspects of the delivery process. The company worked to develop more standardized procedures for its retail partners, including guidelines for order processing and delivery timelines. However, given the wide range of retailers on the platform—many of whom were smaller, independent stores—it was difficult to enforce these standards uniformly. As a result, logistical inefficiencies persisted, especially in regions where Fynd had recently expanded.

The logistical challenges were further exacerbated by the platform's rapid growth. As Fynd onboarded more retailers and expanded into new markets, the complexities of managing deliveries across multiple locations increased. The platform lacked the logistical infrastructure and technology required to scale its operations effectively, leading to a deterioration in service quality. In contrast, larger e-commerce platforms like Amazon and Flipkart had already invested heavily in building sophisticated logistics networks that could handle large-scale operations efficiently. Fynd, on the other hand, struggled to keep up with the demands of its growing customer base, especially as it expanded into more cities.

As Fynd expanded, its logistics network became increasingly fragmented. The platform's decentralized approach meant that it relied on the delivery capabilities of each individual retailer, which varied significantly in quality and efficiency. Some stores were able to handle deliveries effectively, while others lacked the resources or infrastructure to meet customer expectations. This lack of consistency created frustration for users who expected a seamless experience across all stores on the platform but instead encountered varying levels of service depending on which retailer they ordered from.

Moreover, the platform's reliance on third-party delivery services added another layer of complexity to its logistics operations. While Fynd could theoretically offer same-day or next-day delivery, the quality of service from third-party couriers was inconsistent. These couriers were often handling deliveries for multiple clients simultaneously, which led to delayed or missed deliveries for Fynd customers. The lack of control over this critical aspect of the customer experience further eroded trust in the platform.

In addition to these challenges, Fynd also faced difficulties in managing the reverse logistics process, particularly when it came to handling returns and exchanges. Customers who received incorrect or damaged items often faced long delays in getting their orders corrected, as the process of returning items to the store and having replacements dispatched was slow and cumbersome. Unlike larger e-commerce players, which had centralized returns processes and dedicated logistics for handling such issues, Fynd had to rely on each individual store to manage returns, leading to a fragmented and frustrating experience for customers.

Ultimately, the logistical challenges Fynd faced significantly impacted its ability to compete with larger e-commerce platforms. While the O2O model offered a unique value proposition in theory, the practical realities of managing decentralized logistics and delivery networks proved to be a major hurdle. Customers increasingly turned to platforms like Amazon, Flipkart, and Myntra, which could offer faster, more reliable delivery, and a more consistent shopping experience. Fynd's inability to resolve its logistics issues in a scalable way contributed to its decline and eventual failure.

In conclusion, logistics and delivery issues were a major factor in Fynd's downfall. The platform's decentralized approach to fulfillment, reliance on inconsistent third-party couriers, and lack of centralized logistics infrastructure made it difficult to offer the fast, reliable service that customers expected. As Fynd expanded, these issues became more pronounced, leading to customer dissatisfaction and a gradual erosion of trust in the platform. Despite attempts to streamline its operations, Fynd was ultimately unable to overcome the logistical challenges that hindered its growth.

9. Attempts to Innovate

As Fynd faced increasing operational and logistical challenges, the company sought to innovate its platform and introduce new features in an attempt to regain its competitive edge. Fynd's leadership recognized that addressing the inventory and delivery issues alone would not be enough to sustain long-term growth, so they began experimenting with new technology solutions and expanding their product offerings to attract a broader audience.

One of the first innovations Fynd introduced was an enhanced inventory management system. The company developed a proprietary software solution that was designed to streamline the process of updating stock levels in real time. This system was offered to retailers as part of their partnership with Fynd, helping them track their inventory more efficiently and providing more accurate information to customers. While this innovation showed promise in addressing the stock mismatch issues, its adoption was slow, especially among smaller retailers who were resistant to changing their existing processes. As a result, Fynd's inventory problems persisted, limiting the impact of this innovation.

In addition to improving inventory management, Fynd also explored expanding its product categories beyond fashion. The company ventured into offering accessories, footwear, and lifestyle products to diversify its offerings and increase its average order value. The goal was to attract a wider range of customers who might be interested in more than just clothing, creating a more comprehensive shopping experience. However, this expansion into new categories introduced additional complexity in managing inventory and logistics, and Fynd struggled to maintain the same level of service quality across these new product lines.

Another key area of innovation for Fynd was its attempt to leverage technology to improve the customer experience. The company invested in developing advanced algorithms to offer personalized recommendations to users based on their browsing and purchase history. This feature aimed to increase engagement and drive more sales by making it easier for customers to discover products they were likely to be interested in. While the recommendation engine did help improve user engagement, it was not enough to offset the platform's broader operational challenges, and many customers still left the platform due to delivery issues and inconsistent inventory.

Fynd also experimented with offering new services such as in-store pickup, which allowed customers to reserve products online and pick them up directly from the retail store. This feature aimed to bridge the gap between online and offline shopping even further, offering customers the convenience of browsing online with the immediacy of picking up their purchase in person. While this service was well-received by some customers, it did not gain widespread traction, as many users still preferred the convenience of home delivery.

Another innovation Fynd attempted was expanding its partnerships beyond just fashion retailers. The company explored collaborations with other sectors, including electronics and home goods, in an effort to broaden its product offerings and attract a larger customer base. However, this diversification strategy further complicated the logistics of managing real-time inventory updates and deliveries from multiple categories. The challenges of coordinating across different types of retailers made it difficult for Fynd to deliver the same seamless experience in these new categories as it had in fashion.

Fynd also tried to improve its operational efficiency by investing in data analytics. The company began analyzing customer behavior, delivery patterns, and vendor performance to identify areas where it could optimize its operations. By using data to improve decision-making, Fynd hoped to reduce delivery times, minimize stock mismatches, and streamline its logistics processes. However, despite these efforts, the fundamental issues of managing decentralized inventory and delivery networks continued to plague the platform.

In summary, while Fynd made several attempts to innovate and address its operational challenges, these innovations were not enough to overcome the platform's deeper structural issues. The enhanced inventory management system, expanded product categories, and personalized recommendations all showed promise but failed to fully address the logistical bottlenecks and inconsistent service quality that had become major pain points for customers. Fynd's innovations, though well-intentioned, could not keep pace with the scale of the challenges the platform faced as it expanded.

10. Financial Decline

As Fynd continued to grapple with operational, logistical, and competitive pressures, the financial health of the company began to deteriorate. The company's inability to scale its business model efficiently, coupled with its struggles to secure consistent funding, led to mounting financial strain. While Fynd had raised initial rounds of funding, the ongoing operational challenges made it difficult for the company to attract new investors, and the lack of fresh capital further hindered its ability to invest in the infrastructure needed to support its growth.

One of the main financial challenges Fynd faced was the rising cost of logistics. The platform's decentralized delivery model, which relied on individual retailers to fulfill orders, proved to be more expensive than anticipated. Many of Fynd's retail partners lacked the capacity to handle deliveries efficiently, and the platform had to rely on third-party couriers to complete many orders. These delivery costs, combined with the need to coordinate across multiple stores, led to higher-than-expected operational expenses. As Fynd expanded, these costs continued to rise, putting significant pressure on the company's cash flow.

Fynd's financial struggles were also compounded by its inability to maintain a stable revenue stream. While the company saw early success in attracting customers, its operational challenges led to high levels of customer churn. Many users who had initially been attracted to the platform left due to delivery delays, stock mismatches, and inconsistent service quality. This high churn rate made it difficult for Fynd to grow its customer base and achieve the economies of scale needed to offset its rising operational costs. The company's revenue growth stagnated, while its expenses continued to climb, leading to a widening financial gap.

The platform's reliance on external funding to support its growth further exacerbated its financial challenges. As Fynd's operational issues became more apparent, investors grew increasingly hesitant to provide additional capital. The company's inability to demonstrate a clear path to profitability made it difficult to attract new investment, and Fynd was forced to operate with limited resources. Without the necessary capital to invest in improving its logistics infrastructure, expanding its product offerings, or enhancing its technology, Fynd found itself in a vicious cycle of declining service quality and shrinking customer engagement.

Fynd's financial decline was also reflected in its relationships with its retail partners. As the company's cash flow issues worsened, it struggled to make timely payments to its retail partners, leading to strained relationships with some of its most important stakeholders. Retailers who had initially been enthusiastic about partnering with Fynd began to lose confidence in the platform's ability to deliver on its promises, further complicating the company's efforts to maintain its inventory and service quality.

In addition to operational and funding challenges, Fynd faced increasing pressure from competitors, which made it difficult for the platform to generate revenue. Larger players like Amazon, Flipkart, and Myntra continued to dominate the e-commerce market, offering aggressive discounts, faster deliveries, and more extensive product catalogs. These competitors were able to leverage their economies of scale and vast logistical networks to offer lower prices and better service, making it difficult for Fynd to compete on either price or convenience. As a result, Fynd's market share shrank, and its revenue base continued to erode.

Despite efforts to streamline operations and reduce costs, Fynd was unable to reverse its financial decline. The company's operational inefficiencies, coupled with its inability to secure additional funding, made it difficult to invest in the improvements needed to turn the business around. As the financial pressures mounted, Fynd found itself increasingly unable to compete in the highly competitive

Key Points

- **Fynd's business model** aimed to bridge the gap between online and offline retail by offering real-time inventory access from physical stores, but the company struggled to maintain this balance at scale.
- **Inventory management issues** were central to Fynd's challenges, as the platform struggled to provide accurate, real-time stock information, leading to dissatisfied customers and disrupted service.
- **Funding problems** further limited Fynd's growth, as the company faced difficulties raising enough capital to compete with larger e-commerce platforms that dominated both online and offline retail spaces.
- **The competitive landscape** of the retail-tech sector, with giants like Amazon and Flipkart improving their omni-channel strategies, made it difficult for Fynd to carve out a sustainable market position.
- **Fynd's fall** serves as a lesson in the importance of accurate inventory systems, strong operational frameworks, and

sufficient funding when navigating the complex intersection of online and offline retail.

Satyam Tripathi

Chapter 9. Yebhi: The Highs and Lows of Discount-Driven Growth and Inventory Mismanagement

1. Introduction to Yebhi

Yebhi was founded in 2009 with a vision to become a one-stop online destination for lifestyle products, focusing initially on fashion, footwear, and home decor. The platform aimed to capitalize on the growing demand for online shopping in India, which was just beginning to take off at that time. With a consumer base that was increasingly becoming internet-savvy and seeking convenience, Yebhi positioned itself as a platform that offered a wide range of products at competitive prices, catering to the evolving needs of the Indian middle class.

Yebhi's entry into the market came at a time when e-commerce in India was still in its nascent stages. Consumers were just beginning to explore online shopping, and there was significant room for growth. Platforms like Flipkart and Snapdeal had also entered the scene around the same time, but Yebhi sought to differentiate itself by focusing heavily on fashion and lifestyle products. By offering a wide selection of items across categories such as clothing, footwear, accessories, and home decor, Yebhi aimed to capture a broad demographic of consumers.

The company's early success can be attributed to its ability to offer products at deeply discounted prices, which appealed to price-sensitive Indian consumers. Yebhi quickly gained traction, attracting a loyal customer base that was eager to take advantage of the discounts and deals offered on the platform. The brand positioned itself as a discount-driven e-commerce player, focusing on volume sales through competitive pricing. This strategy helped Yebhi build a strong presence in a market that was increasingly looking for affordable options online.

Yebhi's founders, led by Manmohan Agarwal, envisioned the platform as more than just a discount retailer. They saw Yebhi as a lifestyle destination, offering not only fashion but also home goods, electronics, and personal care products. This diverse product range was designed to cater to the various needs of middle-class Indian households. By providing a wide selection of products across different categories, Yebhi hoped to become a household name in e-commerce, offering everything from clothing to furniture at affordable prices.

In the early stages, Yebhi's growth was fueled by a combination of aggressive marketing campaigns and partnerships with local and international brands. The platform onboarded a variety of sellers and manufacturers, allowing it to offer a broad catalog of products. Yebhi's ability to secure partnerships with well-known brands helped boost its credibility among consumers, who were still developing trust in online shopping. By offering recognizable brands at discounted rates, Yebhi was able to build a customer base that valued both variety and affordability.

As the platform gained momentum, Yebhi also invested in building a strong technological infrastructure to support its growing operations. The company focused on creating a user-friendly interface that made it easy for customers to browse products, place orders, and track deliveries. In a market where many consumers were still new to online shopping, having a smooth and seamless user experience was crucial to gaining trust and ensuring repeat business. Yebhi's early investments in technology helped it stand out in a competitive market, where customer experience was becoming increasingly important.

In summary, Yebhi's launch in 2009 marked the beginning of its ambitious journey to capture a significant share of the Indian e-commerce market. By focusing on fashion, home decor, and lifestyle products, and by offering competitive prices, the platform quickly gained traction among consumers. The combination of a wide product range, strong brand partnerships, and a user-friendly interface positioned Yebhi as a key player in the rapidly growing e-commerce sector in India. However, this early success would soon be overshadowed by the operational and financial challenges that the company would face as it scaled.

2. Early Market Entry and Expansion

Yebhi's early entry into the Indian e-commerce market gave it a first-mover advantage, allowing the platform to establish itself as a major player before the space became overcrowded with competitors. The company's decision to focus on fashion and lifestyle products gave it a unique position in the market. Yebhi was able to carve out a niche for itself by offering trendy and affordable products, which resonated with the Indian middle class that was increasingly looking for stylish yet budget-friendly options online.

In its early years, Yebhi expanded rapidly across multiple product categories, moving beyond fashion and footwear to include home decor, electronics, and personal care products. The platform aimed to become a comprehensive lifestyle destination, catering to a wide range of consumer needs. By offering a variety of products at discounted prices, Yebhi was able to appeal to a broad demographic of consumers, from college students looking for affordable fashion to families seeking deals on household items.

One of the key factors that contributed to Yebhi's early success was its aggressive marketing campaigns. The company invested heavily in digital marketing, leveraging social media platforms, email marketing, and online ads to reach its target audience. Yebhi's marketing strategy was focused on highlighting its discounts and deals, which helped attract price-sensitive consumers who were eager to take advantage of the platform's competitive pricing. These campaigns helped Yebhi build brand awareness and drive traffic to its platform, leading to increased sales and customer acquisition.

In addition to its digital marketing efforts, Yebhi also explored offline marketing initiatives to reach a broader audience. The company launched print and TV advertising campaigns, positioning itself as a go-to destination for affordable lifestyle products. By combining both online and offline marketing strategies, Yebhi was able to build a strong brand presence across different consumer segments. This multi-channel approach helped the platform reach consumers who were still new to online shopping and were more comfortable engaging with brands they had seen in traditional media.

Yebhi's rapid expansion into new product categories and its aggressive marketing efforts were complemented by strategic partnerships with manufacturers and brands. The platform onboarded a wide range of local and international brands, giving consumers access to a diverse catalog of products. These partnerships allowed Yebhi to offer exclusive deals and discounts on popular brands, further strengthening its value proposition as a discount-driven platform. By securing these partnerships, Yebhi was able to attract a loyal customer base that valued both variety and affordability.

As Yebhi expanded its product offerings and customer base, the platform also worked on building a robust supply chain and logistics network to support its growing operations. The company partnered with third-party logistics providers to ensure timely deliveries and worked to optimize its warehousing and fulfillment processes. In the early stages,

Yebhi was able to maintain a relatively smooth supply chain, which contributed to its ability to scale quickly. However, as the platform continued to grow, managing inventory and logistics would become increasingly difficult, leading to significant challenges down the line.

Despite its early success, Yebhi's rapid expansion also brought with it several risks. The platform's reliance on heavy discounting to drive sales meant that its profit margins were thin, and as the company scaled, it struggled to balance growth with profitability. Additionally, the fast-paced expansion into new product categories and regions stretched the company's resources thin, leading to operational inefficiencies that would later contribute to its decline. While Yebhi's early market entry and expansion helped it gain a foothold in the e-commerce space, the challenges of managing this growth would soon catch up with the platform.

3. Business Model and Competitive Landscape

Yebhi's business model was centered around offering deeply discounted products across a wide range of categories, including fashion, footwear, home decor, and electronics. The platform's focus on providing affordable options for price-sensitive consumers became its core value proposition, allowing it to compete in a market where customers were highly motivated by discounts and deals. Yebhi's strategy was to drive sales volume through heavy discounting, relying on economies of scale to achieve profitability. However, while this model helped Yebhi grow rapidly in its early years, it also came with significant challenges.

One of the key aspects of Yebhi's business model was its reliance on securing inventory from manufacturers and wholesalers at discounted rates. The platform worked with a variety of suppliers, purchasing products in bulk to negotiate lower prices. These cost savings were then passed on to customers in the form of discounts, which helped attract a large number of consumers looking for deals. Yebhi's ability to offer significant discounts on popular brands was a major driver of customer acquisition, and the platform's sales volumes grew quickly as a result.

However, this discount-driven model also meant that Yebhi's profit margins were razor-thin. The company was operating on a high-volume, low-margin basis, which made it vulnerable to fluctuations in demand and rising operational costs. While the discounts helped attract customers, they also created an expectation that Yebhi would consistently offer the lowest prices in the market. This reliance on discounting made it difficult for the platform to build a sustainable business model, as it struggled to balance growth with profitability.

Yebhi's business model also positioned it in direct competition with other e-commerce players that were entering the market around the same time. Platforms like Flipkart, Snapdeal, and Myntra were also offering discounts and deals to attract customers, creating a highly competitive environment in the Indian e-commerce space. While Yebhi initially differentiated itself by focusing on lifestyle products and fashion, the increasing overlap in product categories with other platforms made it harder for Yebhi to maintain a competitive edge. As these competitors scaled their operations and secured larger funding rounds, Yebhi found itself struggling to keep up.

The competitive landscape was further intensified by the entry of international players like Amazon, which brought significant resources and expertise to the Indian market. Amazon's vast product catalog, advanced logistics network, and ability to offer aggressive discounts made it a formidable competitor for Yebhi. As these larger players continued to gain market share, Yebhi's position in the market became increasingly precarious. The platform's reliance on discounts to drive sales was no longer enough to compete with the operational efficiencies and customer loyalty programs offered by its competitors.

In addition to competing with e-commerce giants, Yebhi also faced competition from smaller, niche players that specialized in specific product categories. For example, platforms like Jabong and Zivame focused exclusively on fashion and lingerie, respectively, offering a more tailored shopping experience for customers in these categories. Yebhi's attempt to be a one-stop-shop for lifestyle products meant that it was competing on multiple fronts, which diluted its ability to focus on any one category. This lack of specialization made it harder for Yebhi to stand out in a crowded market, where customers were increasingly looking for curated shopping experiences.

Despite these challenges, Yebhi continued to pursue its discount-driven growth strategy, doubling down on its efforts to attract customers through aggressive marketing and promotions. However, as the competitive landscape became more intense and the platform's operational inefficiencies began to surface, it became clear that Yebhi's business model was not sustainable in the long run. The company's reliance on discounts, coupled with its inability to compete effectively with larger players, would ultimately contribute to its downfall.

4. Heavy Discounting Strategy

Yebhi's heavy discounting strategy played a central role in its early success, as it allowed the platform to quickly attract a large number of customers. The Indian e-commerce market, particularly in its early stages, was characterized by price-sensitive consumers who were looking for the best deals. Yebhi capitalized on this by offering deep discounts on a wide range of products, making it an attractive destination for shoppers looking to save money. The platform's discount-driven approach helped it grow rapidly, but it also created several long-term challenges for the company.

The foundation of Yebhi's discounting strategy was its ability to purchase inventory in bulk from manufacturers and wholesalers at lower prices. By securing products at discounted rates, Yebhi was able to offer significant price reductions to consumers. These discounts often ranged from 20% to 70% off the retail price, which made Yebhi a go-to destination for deal-hunters. The platform's aggressive pricing helped it stand out in a competitive market, and its sales volumes grew quickly as more and more customers flocked to the site in search of bargains.

One of the key advantages of this discounting strategy was that it helped Yebhi build a large customer base in a relatively short period of time. In a market where online shopping was still a relatively new concept, offering deep discounts was an effective way to encourage consumers to try the platform. Yebhi's marketing campaigns heavily promoted these discounts, using slogans and ads that emphasized the savings customers could achieve by shopping on the platform. This messaging resonated with consumers who were looking for affordable options, particularly in the fashion and home decor categories.

However, while Yebhi's discounting strategy helped drive customer acquisition, it also created an expectation among consumers that the platform would always offer the lowest prices. As a result, many customers became highly price-sensitive, choosing to shop on Yebhi only when discounts were available. This created a reliance on sales promotions and discount events to drive traffic to the site. While these promotions helped boost short-term sales, they also eroded the platform's ability to generate sustainable revenue. Yebhi found itself in a position where it had to constantly offer discounts to maintain its customer base, which put pressure on its already thin profit margins.

The heavy discounting also made it difficult for Yebhi to differentiate itself from its competitors. Other e-commerce platforms, such as Flipkart and Snapdeal, were also offering discounts and deals to attract customers. As a result, the e-commerce market became a race to the bottom, with platforms competing on price rather than product quality or service. Yebhi's reliance on discounts made it vulnerable to competition from larger players who had more resources to sustain aggressive pricing strategies. While Yebhi was able to offer discounts in the short term, it struggled to maintain this strategy as operational costs increased and profit margins shrank.

Moreover, the discounting strategy had a negative impact on Yebhi's relationships with suppliers and manufacturers. In order to maintain its low prices, Yebhi often had to negotiate for better deals from its suppliers, which put strain on these relationships. As the platform scaled, it became increasingly difficult to secure inventory at the same discounted rates, which led to supply chain issues and stock shortages. This, in turn, affected Yebhi's ability to fulfill customer orders, leading to delays and dissatisfaction among shoppers.

In conclusion, while Yebhi's heavy discounting strategy helped the platform achieve rapid growth in its early years, it also created a number of challenges that ultimately contributed to its decline. The reliance on discounts made it difficult for Yebhi to build a sustainable business model, and the platform struggled to compete with larger players who could afford to offer aggressive pricing over the long term. Additionally, the strain on supplier relationships and the negative impact on profit margins further weakened Yebhi's position in the market.

5. Inventory Management Issues

As Yebhi grew and expanded into more product categories, managing inventory became one of its biggest challenges. The platform's business model relied on offering a wide range of products at discounted rates, but this strategy placed immense pressure on its inventory management system. Yebhi struggled to keep track of stock levels across different categories and vendors, which led to frequent stock mismatches and product unavailability. These issues significantly affected the customer experience, as shoppers often found that the items they had ordered were either out of stock or delayed due to inventory problems.

The platform's rapid expansion made it increasingly difficult to manage inventory across multiple categories like fashion, home decor, footwear, and electronics. Yebhi's business model involved sourcing products from various manufacturers and wholesalers, which required the company to maintain an accurate and up-to-date inventory. However, as the number of vendors and products increased, Yebhi's ability to maintain an organized and efficient inventory system diminished. The company's infrastructure was not equipped to handle the complexities of tracking inventory across multiple suppliers, resulting in frequent inaccuracies.

One of the key problems Yebhi faced was the inability to synchronize its inventory data with its suppliers in real time. Many suppliers did not have the technological capabilities to update their stock levels regularly, which meant that Yebhi's platform often displayed products that were no longer available. This led to a situation where customers placed orders for items that appeared to be in stock, only to be informed later that the product was unavailable. This not only caused frustration among customers but also damaged Yebhi's reputation as a reliable e-commerce platform.

The inventory management issues were further compounded by Yebhi's reliance on third-party logistics providers for order fulfillment. As Yebhi scaled, the company outsourced much of its warehousing and delivery operations to external partners. While this helped reduce operational costs, it also created additional challenges in maintaining control over the supply chain. The lack of integration between Yebhi's inventory system and its logistics partners made it difficult to track orders and ensure that products were delivered on time. Delays in order processing and shipping became increasingly common, leading to higher rates of customer dissatisfaction.

In addition to stock mismatches and delivery delays, Yebhi also faced challenges in managing returns and exchanges. The platform's discount-driven strategy meant that many customers were purchasing items on impulse, leading to higher return rates. However, Yebhi's inventory management system was not designed to handle the influx of returns efficiently. Products that were returned often took longer to be processed and restocked, further complicating the already strained inventory system. This not only impacted Yebhi's ability to fulfill new orders but also increased the company's operational costs.

The inventory management issues also affected Yebhi's relationships with suppliers. As the platform struggled to maintain accurate stock levels, suppliers became frustrated with the frequent order cancellations and delays in payments. Many suppliers began to view Yebhi as an unreliable partner, which made it difficult for the company to negotiate better deals or secure exclusive inventory. The strained relationships with suppliers contributed to Yebhi's declining ability to offer the same variety of products at discounted rates, further eroding its competitive advantage.

In conclusion, Yebhi's poor inventory management was a significant factor in the platform's decline. The company's inability to track stock levels accurately, coupled with its reliance on third-party logistics providers, led to frequent stock mismatches, delivery delays, and customer dissatisfaction. As Yebhi continued to expand, these issues only worsened, creating a vicious cycle of operational inefficiencies and lost business. The failure to invest in a robust inventory management system ultimately undermined Yebhi's ability to scale and compete in the increasingly competitive e-commerce landscape.

6. Operational Struggles

As Yebhi grew rapidly, the company faced significant operational struggles that ultimately hindered its ability to scale effectively. While the platform's aggressive discounting strategy helped attract customers, it also placed immense pressure on Yebhi's supply chain and logistics operations. The company's rapid expansion into new categories and regions stretched its resources thin, leading to inefficiencies in order fulfillment, warehousing, and delivery. These operational challenges became increasingly difficult to manage as Yebhi attempted to keep pace with competitors in the e-commerce space.

One of the key operational challenges Yebhi faced was the management of its supply chain. As the company expanded its product offerings, it needed to coordinate with a growing number of suppliers and vendors to source inventory. However, Yebhi's supply chain infrastructure was not designed to handle the complexities of managing such a diverse range of products. The company struggled to ensure that products were sourced, stocked, and delivered in a timely manner, leading to frequent delays and stockouts. The lack of integration between Yebhi's suppliers and its internal systems exacerbated these issues, making it difficult to maintain an efficient flow of goods.

In addition to supply chain issues, Yebhi also faced challenges in warehousing and order fulfillment. The platform relied on a network of third-party logistics providers to manage its warehousing operations, but the lack of standardization across these providers led to inconsistencies in how orders were processed and shipped. Some warehouses were more efficient than others, leading to uneven delivery times for customers. This fragmentation of Yebhi's logistics network made it difficult to maintain a consistent level of service, particularly as the company expanded into new regions.

The outsourcing of logistics operations also created challenges in terms of quality control. As Yebhi scaled, it became increasingly reliant on external partners to manage key aspects of its business, including warehousing, packaging, and delivery. However, the company struggled to enforce quality standards across its logistics network, resulting in frequent issues with damaged products, incorrect orders, and delayed deliveries. These operational inefficiencies led to a growing number of customer complaints, which further eroded Yebhi's reputation as a reliable e-commerce platform.

Another significant operational challenge was managing the high volume of returns and exchanges. Yebhi's discount-driven strategy attracted a large number of customers who were motivated by low prices but often returned products due to dissatisfaction with quality or fit. The platform's return rate was higher than anticipated, and Yebhi's logistics infrastructure was not equipped to handle the influx of returned products efficiently. This created bottlenecks in the supply chain, as returned items took longer to process and restock, further straining Yebhi's ability to fulfill new orders.

In an attempt to address its operational struggles, Yebhi made several efforts to streamline its logistics and supply chain operations. The company invested in upgrading its technology infrastructure, with a focus on improving inventory management and order tracking systems. Yebhi also sought to renegotiate contracts with its logistics partners to improve delivery times and reduce costs. However, these efforts were not enough to resolve the underlying issues, and Yebhi continued to face challenges in maintaining operational efficiency as it scaled.

The operational struggles also had a direct impact on Yebhi's ability to compete with larger players in the e-commerce space. While platforms like Amazon and Flipkart had invested heavily in building their own logistics networks, Yebhi's reliance on third-party providers left it at a disadvantage. The company lacked the logistical capabilities to offer the same level of service as its competitors, particularly when it came to delivery speed and order accuracy. As a result, Yebhi found itself losing customers to platforms that could offer a more seamless and reliable shopping experience.

In conclusion, Yebhi's operational struggles were a major contributor to the platform's decline. The company's inability to manage its supply chain, warehousing, and logistics effectively led to delays, stockouts, and a growing number of customer complaints. Despite efforts to address these issues, Yebhi was unable to scale its operations efficiently, which ultimately limited its ability to compete with larger e-commerce platforms. The operational inefficiencies, combined with the platform's reliance on discounts to drive sales, made it difficult for Yebhi to maintain its early success as the market became more competitive.

7. Funding and Financial Challenges

Despite Yebhi's early success and rapid growth, the company faced significant financial challenges that made it difficult to sustain its operations. Yebhi raised several rounds of funding from investors who were eager to capitalize on the booming e-commerce market in India. However, the company's reliance on deep discounts and aggressive marketing campaigns to attract customers meant that its profit margins were extremely thin. As a result, Yebhi struggled to achieve profitability, even as its sales volumes increased.

One of the key financial challenges Yebhi faced was its high customer acquisition costs. The company invested heavily in digital and offline marketing campaigns to drive traffic to its platform and attract new customers. While these campaigns helped boost sales in the short term, they also resulted in significant expenses that ate into Yebhi's already thin profit margins. The company's reliance on discounts further compounded this issue, as many customers were drawn to the platform specifically for the low prices and were unlikely to make repeat purchases without similar discounts.

Yebhi's financial difficulties were exacerbated by its operational inefficiencies. The company's struggles with inventory management, order fulfillment, and logistics led to higher operating costs, which further strained its finances. Yebhi was forced to spend more on resolving customer complaints, processing returns, and managing stockouts, all of which added to its overall expenses. As these operational issues persisted, the company found it increasingly difficult to control its costs and improve its bottom line.

In an attempt to address its financial challenges, Yebhi sought to raise additional funding from investors. The company raised multiple rounds of funding from venture capital firms, including Nexus Venture Partners, who believed in the platform's potential to become a major player in the Indian e-commerce market. However, as Yebhi continued to struggle with profitability, investors grew increasingly concerned about the platform's ability to sustain its growth. The company's financial performance failed to meet investor expectations, and Yebhi found it difficult to raise new capital as a result.

Another factor that contributed to Yebhi's financial challenges was its inability to build customer loyalty. While the platform's discount-driven strategy helped attract a large number of customers, many of these customers were price-sensitive and primarily motivated by the deals Yebhi offered. As a result, customer retention rates were low, and Yebhi had to constantly invest in marketing and discounts to drive repeat purchases. This made it difficult for the company to generate consistent revenue and achieve economies of scale.

In addition to its struggles with profitability, Yebhi also faced challenges in managing its cash flow. The company's high return rates and operational inefficiencies meant that it often had to issue refunds to customers, which further strained its finances. Yebhi's reliance on third-party logistics providers also meant that the company had limited control over its delivery costs, which fluctuated depending on the volume of orders. These cash flow issues made it difficult for Yebhi to manage its day-to-day operations and pay its suppliers on time, leading to strained relationships with vendors.

Despite efforts to cut costs and improve its financial performance, Yebhi was unable to achieve the profitability required to sustain its operations. The company's high customer acquisition costs, thin profit margins, and operational inefficiencies created a financial burden that Yebhi could not overcome. As the e-commerce market became more competitive and larger players like Amazon and Flipkart continued to grow, Yebhi found itself unable to compete on price, service, or operational efficiency.

In conclusion, Yebhi's financial challenges were a major factor in its eventual decline. The company's reliance on discounts to drive sales, coupled with its high customer acquisition costs and operational inefficiencies, made it difficult for Yebhi to achieve profitability. Despite raising several rounds of funding, the company was unable to sustain its growth and faced increasing pressure from investors to improve its financial performance. Ultimately, Yebhi's financial struggles, combined with its operational issues, limited its ability to compete effectively in the e-commerce space.

8. Decline in Market Share

As Yebhi faced mounting operational and financial challenges, the platform began to lose market share to competitors who were better equipped to scale efficiently and provide a seamless shopping experience. The entry of global e-commerce giants like Amazon, coupled with the aggressive expansion of local players like Flipkart and Myntra, made it increasingly difficult for Yebhi to maintain its position in the market. These competitors not only had deeper pockets, but they also invested heavily in logistics, inventory management, and customer service, areas where Yebhi struggled to keep up.

One of the key reasons for Yebhi’s declining market share was its inability to offer the same level of customer service as its competitors. Platforms like Amazon and Flipkart had established sophisticated logistics networks that allowed them to offer fast and reliable deliveries, while Yebhi continued to grapple with delays, stock mismatches, and inconsistent service quality. As customers became more accustomed to faster delivery times and hassle-free shopping experiences on other platforms, many began to shift away from Yebhi in favor of competitors who could provide a more reliable service.

Another major factor contributing to Yebhi’s decline was the rise of Myntra, which focused exclusively on fashion and lifestyle products—Yebhi’s core product categories. Myntra, with its superior logistics infrastructure and ability to secure exclusive brand partnerships, quickly became the go-to destination for fashion-conscious consumers. Myntra's investments in technology and user experience allowed it to offer a more personalized shopping journey, something Yebhi struggled to achieve as it expanded across multiple categories. The shift in consumer preference towards specialized platforms like Myntra further eroded Yebhi's market share.

The growing influence of Amazon in the Indian market also posed a significant challenge to Yebhi. Amazon's global expertise in logistics and inventory management, combined with its ability to offer aggressive pricing and vast product selections, gave it a considerable advantage over local competitors. As Amazon expanded its operations in India, it quickly gained traction among consumers who were attracted to its competitive prices, fast deliveries, and customer-friendly policies. Yebhi, with its limited resources, could not compete on the same scale, and many customers who had initially shopped on Yebhi began to migrate to Amazon for their online shopping needs.

In addition to competition from larger players, Yebhi also faced challenges from niche platforms that specialized in specific categories. For example, platforms like Pepperfry, which focused on furniture and home decor, began to capture a significant share of the home goods market, one of Yebhi's key product categories. Similarly, other specialized e-commerce platforms like Jabong and Limeroad carved out their own niches in the fashion sector, further fragmenting the market and reducing Yebhi's share. Yebhi's attempt to be a one-stop-shop for lifestyle products ultimately worked against it, as consumers increasingly gravitated towards platforms that offered a more focused and curated shopping experience.

As Yebhi's market share declined, the company's financial situation worsened. The platform's reliance on heavy discounting to attract customers became unsustainable as its operational costs continued to rise. Unlike its larger competitors, Yebhi did not have the financial backing to maintain its discount-driven strategy in the face of declining sales. The combination of dwindling revenue, high operational costs, and increasing competition left Yebhi in a precarious financial position, with little room for recovery.

In an effort to stem the decline, Yebhi made several attempts to refocus its strategy. The company tried to scale back its discounting efforts and emphasize the quality and variety of its product offerings. However, by this time, Yebhi's competitors had already solidified their positions in the market, making it difficult for Yebhi to regain lost ground. Consumers who had switched to platforms like Amazon, Flipkart, and Myntra were unlikely to return, given the superior service and reliability offered by these platforms.

In conclusion, Yebhi's decline in market share was the result of increased competition from both global and local players who were able to scale their operations more efficiently and offer a better customer experience. Yebhi's inability to keep pace with these competitors, coupled with its ongoing operational and financial struggles, led to a steady erosion of its market position. The platform's reliance on discounts, without addressing its underlying operational inefficiencies, ultimately proved to be an unsustainable strategy in a rapidly evolving e-commerce landscape.

9. Attempts to Revive the Platform

As Yebhi's market share continued to decline and financial pressures mounted, the company made several attempts to revive the platform and regain its competitive edge. The leadership team recognized that the heavy discounting strategy, while effective in driving initial growth, had become a liability as operational costs rose and profit margins shrank. In response, Yebhi sought to refocus its efforts on improving operational efficiency, expanding its product offerings, and enhancing the overall customer experience.

One of Yebhi's first attempts at revival was to reduce its reliance on discounts and promotions. The company realized that constantly offering deep discounts was not a sustainable way to drive growth, especially as competitors like Amazon and Flipkart could afford to offer similar deals without compromising profitability. Yebhi began to emphasize the quality of its products, positioning itself as a platform that offered value for money rather than just low prices. The goal was to shift consumer perception and attract more price-insensitive customers who were willing to pay for quality.

In tandem with this shift in strategy, Yebhi made efforts to improve its inventory management and logistics operations. The company recognized that one of its biggest challenges was the frequent stock mismatches and delivery delays that frustrated customers. Yebhi invested in upgrading its technology infrastructure, including developing a more robust inventory management system that could track stock levels in real time. The company also sought to improve its partnerships with third-party logistics providers to ensure faster and more reliable deliveries.

Yebhi also explored new product categories in an attempt to diversify its revenue streams. The platform expanded into categories like electronics, personal care, and kitchen appliances, hoping to attract a broader range of customers. The idea was to reduce Yebhi's dependence on fashion and lifestyle products, which were already dominated by specialized platforms like Myntra. By offering a wider variety of products, Yebhi hoped to increase its average order value and boost sales across different categories.

Despite these efforts, Yebhi struggled to regain the trust of its customers. Many shoppers had been turned off by the platform's previous issues with inventory management and delivery delays, and convincing them to return proved difficult. Competitors like Amazon and Flipkart had set a new standard for customer service, offering fast deliveries, easy returns, and extensive product selections. Yebhi's improvements in these areas, while significant, were not enough to close the gap between the platform and its larger rivals.

In a bid to further revive the platform, Yebhi explored partnerships with international brands and manufacturers. The company aimed to offer exclusive products that could not be found on other e-commerce platforms, hoping that this would give it a competitive edge. However, securing these partnerships proved difficult, as many international brands preferred to work with larger, more established platforms like Amazon and Myntra, which had the logistics capabilities and customer base to support higher sales volumes.

Yebhi also considered pivoting its business model to focus more on being a marketplace rather than a retailer. By allowing third-party sellers to list their products on the platform, Yebhi could reduce the burden of managing inventory and logistics, shifting those responsibilities to the sellers. However, this pivot came too late to make a significant impact, as other platforms like Flipkart and Snapdeal had already established themselves as leading marketplaces in India.

Ultimately, Yebhi's attempts to revive the platform were not enough to reverse its downward trajectory. While the company made commendable efforts to address its operational inefficiencies and expand its product offerings, the competitive landscape had shifted dramatically, leaving little room for Yebhi to make a comeback. The platform's inability to regain customer trust and compete effectively with larger players led to its eventual shutdown.

In conclusion, Yebhi made several strategic attempts to revive the platform, including reducing its reliance on discounts, improving inventory management, and expanding into new product categories. However, these efforts were not enough to counteract the platform's declining market share, financial struggles, and competition from larger players. Yebhi's failure to adapt quickly enough to the evolving e-commerce landscape ultimately sealed its fate.

10. Lessons from Yebhi's Fall

The story of Yebhi offers several key lessons for e-commerce platforms and startups looking to scale in a highly competitive market. One of the most important takeaways is the danger of relying too heavily on discounts to drive growth. While discounting can be an effective strategy for attracting customers in the short term, it is not a sustainable way to build a profitable business. Yebhi's reliance on deep discounts led to thin profit margins, which made it difficult for the platform to invest in critical areas like inventory management, logistics, and customer service.

Another key lesson from Yebhi's fall is the importance of operational efficiency. As Yebhi expanded rapidly, the company struggled to manage its supply chain, warehousing, and order fulfillment processes. The frequent stock mismatches and delivery delays that resulted from these operational inefficiencies led to customer dissatisfaction and ultimately contributed to Yebhi's decline. For e-commerce platforms, ensuring that operational processes can scale alongside growth is essential for maintaining customer satisfaction and long-term success.

Yebhi's failure also highlights the importance of building a sustainable and differentiated value proposition. While Yebhi initially carved out a niche for itself in the fashion and lifestyle space, it failed to differentiate itself from competitors as the market became more crowded. Platforms like Myntra, which focused exclusively on fashion, were able to offer a more tailored and curated shopping experience, while larger players like Amazon and Flipkart provided a broader selection of products with superior logistics and customer service. Yebhi's attempt to be a one-stop-shop for lifestyle products ultimately diluted its focus and made it harder for the platform to stand out.

The story of Yebhi also underscores the importance of maintaining strong relationships with suppliers and logistics partners. Yebhi's operational struggles were exacerbated by its strained relationships with suppliers, many of whom became frustrated with the platform's frequent order cancellations and delayed payments. For e-commerce platforms, building and maintaining trust with suppliers is critical for ensuring a reliable and efficient supply chain. Without strong supplier relationships, platforms risk facing inventory shortages, stock mismatches, and delivery delays that can erode customer trust.

Finally, Yebhi's experience demonstrates the importance of adaptability in a rapidly evolving market. The Indian e-commerce landscape changed dramatically in the years following Yebhi's launch, with the entry of global players like Amazon and the rise of specialized platforms like Myntra and Pepperfry. While Yebhi made several attempts to adapt to these changes, its efforts came too late to make a significant impact. For startups in fast-growing industries, the ability to pivot quickly and respond to market trends is critical for staying competitive and avoiding obsolescence.

In conclusion, Yebhi's fall offers valuable lessons for e-commerce startups and businesses. The platform's reliance on discounts, operational inefficiencies, lack of differentiation, and inability to adapt to a changing market ultimately led to its decline. For e-commerce platforms looking to succeed in a competitive market, building a sustainable business model, investing in operational efficiency, and maintaining strong supplier relationships are key to long-term success.

Key Points

- **Yebhi's growth strategy** relied heavily on deep discounts and aggressive promotions to attract customers, which drove early success but led to unsustainable financial practices over time.

- **Inventory mismanagement** was a critical issue for Yebhi, as the platform struggled to balance stock levels, leading to overstocking and understocking problems that disrupted sales and customer satisfaction.

- **The discount-driven model** eroded profit margins, making it difficult for Yebhi to achieve profitability despite its large customer base, as it could not sustain operations solely through volume.

- **Increased competition** from larger e-commerce players like Flipkart and Snapdeal, who offered similar discounts but with better logistics and inventory systems, made it harder for Yebhi to retain market share.

- **Yebhi's failure** underscores the risks of over-relying on discounts for growth without efficient inventory management and a clear path to profitability, offering a cautionary tale for future e-commerce ventures.

Satyam Tripathi

Chapter 10. Zeppery: Struggles with Partnerships and User Adoption in the Food Tech Revolution

1. Introduction to Zeppery

Zeppery was introduced to the Indian market as an innovative food-tech platform aimed at enhancing the dining experience for customers and restaurants alike. Founded with a vision of simplifying the restaurant-going process, the platform allowed users to pre-order meals and reserve tables before arriving at the restaurant. This not only promised to reduce wait times but also aimed to provide a seamless, efficient dining experience. Zeppery positioned itself as a solution to the time-consuming aspects of dining out, particularly in busy urban environments where popular restaurants often had long queues.

The platform was designed to leverage technology to streamline the customer journey, from selecting a restaurant and reserving a table to pre-ordering meals and paying in advance. This concept was relatively new to the Indian food-tech market, which was largely dominated by food delivery services such as Swiggy and Zomato. Zeppery sought to cater to a different segment of consumers—those who preferred dining out but were frustrated by the inefficiencies that typically accompany it, such as long wait times for both tables and food service.

In the early stages, Zeppery gained some attention as part of the broader food-tech revolution sweeping across India. The platform's founders were confident that integrating digital solutions into the dining experience would appeal to urban professionals, families, and groups looking for more convenience. Zeppery was marketed as a tool to enhance restaurant visits, promising users a hassle-free experience. By allowing customers to pre-order meals, Zeppery aimed to reduce the time spent waiting for food after being seated, a common pain point for diners in crowded cities.

The platform launched with an easy-to-use mobile app that allowed users to browse restaurant menus, make reservations, and order meals in advance. This feature was seen as a significant step towards modernizing the restaurant industry, aligning with the growing trend of integrating technology into everyday activities. At a time when food delivery apps were already transforming the way people consumed food, Zeppery aimed to focus on those who still valued the experience of dining out but sought to make it more efficient and enjoyable.

While the idea behind Zeppery was innovative and catered to a specific need in the market, it also presented a number of challenges. The food-tech space in India was already crowded, and Zeppery's success depended heavily on its ability to form strong partnerships with restaurants, ensure a smooth user experience, and differentiate itself from larger players in the space. The concept of pre-ordering food at restaurants had potential, but its widespread adoption required significant changes in both consumer behavior and restaurant operations.

As Zeppery attempted to carve out its niche, the platform faced numerous obstacles, including limited partnerships with restaurants, low user adoption, and competition from well-established food delivery services. These challenges ultimately prevented Zeppery from scaling as quickly as its founders had hoped, leading to financial struggles and the platform's eventual decline. In hindsight, Zeppery's journey offers valuable lessons about the importance of securing strong partnerships and understanding market dynamics when introducing new technology-driven solutions.

2. Business Model and Market Entry

Zeppery's business model was built around the concept of streamlining the dining experience by allowing customers to pre-order food and reserve tables at restaurants through its mobile app. The company envisioned a future where diners could walk into a restaurant, sit down, and have their food delivered within minutes, having already placed their orders in advance. By reducing wait times and providing a seamless experience, Zeppery aimed to cater to busy professionals, families, and large groups who often faced delays when dining out at popular restaurants.

The primary revenue model for Zeppery was based on commissions from restaurant partners. Each time a customer used the platform to reserve a table or pre-order a meal, the restaurant would pay a percentage of the transaction to Zeppery. This commission-based model was similar to that used by food delivery platforms but focused on dine-in experiences rather than home delivery. Zeppery also explored potential partnerships with restaurants for exclusive promotions, such as offering discounts to customers who ordered through the app, to further incentivize both restaurants and users.

When Zeppery entered the Indian market, the food-tech industry was already booming, primarily driven by the success of food delivery platforms like Swiggy and Zomato. However, Zeppery chose to focus on a different aspect of the dining experience, targeting consumers who preferred to dine out but were looking for ways to make the process more convenient. The platform's founders believed there was untapped potential in this segment, especially in urban areas where people valued both efficiency and quality dining experiences.

Zeppery's market entry was supported by a marketing campaign aimed at educating consumers about the benefits of pre-ordering meals and making reservations in advance. The company highlighted how its platform could help diners save time, avoid long queues, and enjoy a more relaxed dining experience. The messaging was particularly geared towards busy urban professionals who were used to convenience in other areas of their lives—such as through ride-sharing apps or online shopping—but still faced inefficiencies when dining out.

While the concept was promising, Zeppery faced significant challenges from the outset. One of the key hurdles was convincing restaurants to partner with the platform. Unlike food delivery services, which directly increased restaurant revenue by driving home-delivery sales, Zeppery's value proposition was less clear to many restaurateurs. For Zeppery's business model to work, restaurants needed to integrate its technology into their operations, which required additional resources, training, and a willingness to adopt new processes.

Zeppery's limited partnerships with restaurants hampered its ability to scale. Without a broad range of participating restaurants, the platform struggled to attract a critical mass of users. Consumers who were interested in using Zeppery often found that their favorite restaurants were not available on the platform, reducing the app's appeal. This lack of restaurant options created a vicious cycle: fewer partnerships meant fewer users, and fewer users made it harder for Zeppery to secure more restaurant partnerships. This challenge became a major barrier to the platform's growth and long-term success.

3. Partnerships with Restaurants

Zeppery's business model was heavily reliant on forming partnerships with restaurants, as the platform's core functionality—allowing customers to pre-order food and reserve tables—required close collaboration with the restaurant industry. In order for Zeppery to succeed, restaurants needed to adopt the platform's technology, update their processes to accommodate pre-ordered meals, and ensure that their customers received the promised experience. However, securing these partnerships proved to be far more difficult than Zeppery had anticipated.

One of the main challenges Zeppery faced was convincing restaurants of the value that the platform could offer. Many restaurant owners and managers were skeptical about the benefits of integrating pre-ordering technology into their operations. While food delivery platforms like Swiggy and Zomato had demonstrated clear value by driving additional sales through home delivery, Zeppery's model was less straightforward. Pre-ordering was a relatively new concept in the Indian dining landscape, and many restaurateurs were unsure if it would lead to increased foot traffic or higher revenue.

Another challenge was the technical complexity involved in integrating Zeppery's system with the existing operations of restaurants. Many smaller restaurants lacked the technological infrastructure to seamlessly implement pre-ordering systems. Larger restaurants, while more tech-savvy, were often reluctant to make changes to their established processes. For Zeppery to work, restaurants had to update their menus in real-time, ensure that pre-ordered meals were prepared and served promptly, and coordinate with staff to manage both in-house diners and Zeppery customers. This required significant effort and resources, which many restaurants were not willing to invest.

As a result, Zeppery struggled to secure partnerships with well-known or high-traffic restaurants. The platform initially signed up smaller, niche restaurants, but these partnerships did not generate the volume of business needed to attract a large user base. While these restaurants appreciated the potential to streamline operations and reduce wait times for customers, they often lacked the brand recognition or popularity to draw significant traffic to the platform. Without big-name restaurant partnerships, Zeppery found it difficult to market itself as a must-have app for diners.

Another issue Zeppery encountered was competition from other platforms that were also vying for partnerships with restaurants. Food delivery platforms like Swiggy and Zomato had already established strong relationships with restaurants, offering them a reliable source of delivery revenue. Restaurants were more inclined to prioritize partnerships with platforms that directly contributed to their bottom line through delivery sales. In contrast, Zeppery's promise of improving the in-house dining experience was seen as less critical, especially when most restaurants were already operating at capacity during peak hours.

Zeppery's limited ability to secure partnerships with popular restaurants created a significant barrier to scaling the platform. Without enough participating restaurants, the app offered limited choices to users, reducing its overall appeal. Many consumers who downloaded the app found that their preferred restaurants were not available, leading them to abandon the platform. This lack of restaurant variety also hurt Zeppery's ability to expand into new cities and regions, as the platform needed a strong base of local restaurant partners to offer a compelling service in each new market.

6. Competition in the Food Tech Space

Zeppery entered the food tech industry at a time when the market was already crowded with established players, particularly in the food delivery sector. Platforms like Swiggy, Zomato, and Foodpanda had built large user bases and strong restaurant partnerships, making it difficult for new entrants like Zeppery to stand out. The competitive pressure from these larger platforms played a major role in Zeppery's struggles, as it found itself vying for attention in an already saturated market.

Swiggy and Zomato, in particular, had secured dominant positions in the food-tech space by offering a wide range of services, including home delivery, restaurant listings, and even table reservation features. Their comprehensive approach to food-related services allowed them to cater to various consumer needs, from those who wanted food delivered to their doorsteps to those looking for restaurant recommendations. In contrast, Zeppery's niche focus on pre-ordering food for dine-in experiences seemed limited in comparison, especially since its competitors were able to offer similar features alongside delivery services.

Zeppery's primary differentiator—the ability to pre-order meals and reserve tables—did not resonate strongly with users, especially when compared to the convenience of home delivery that was already being offered by competitors. While reducing wait times at restaurants was an appealing concept, it did not address as urgent a need as food delivery, which allowed consumers to enjoy restaurant-quality food from the comfort of their homes. The convenience of food delivery platforms made them more popular with users, leaving Zeppery struggling to find its footing.

In addition to competing for users, Zeppery also faced stiff competition for restaurant partnerships. Swiggy and Zomato had already built extensive networks of restaurant partners, giving them a significant advantage in securing deals with popular restaurants. These platforms offered restaurants a clear value proposition by driving significant sales through home delivery, which increased restaurant revenue without requiring major operational changes. In contrast, Zeppery's model required restaurants to make adjustments to their in-house processes, which made it less attractive to many potential partners.

The competitive landscape was also shaped by the financial backing of Zeppery's rivals. Platforms like Swiggy and Zomato had raised substantial amounts of funding from investors, allowing them to invest heavily in marketing, technology, and logistics. These resources enabled them to scale rapidly, improve their user experience, and offer aggressive discounts to attract more customers. Zeppery, with its limited funding, could not match the financial muscle of its competitors, making it difficult to keep up with their rapid growth and customer acquisition strategies.

Zeppery's inability to differentiate itself from competitors further compounded its challenges. While pre-ordering food was a unique offering, it was not enough to set Zeppery apart in a meaningful way. The app's limited restaurant options and relatively niche appeal meant that it struggled to convince users to adopt it as their go-to dining platform. In contrast, Swiggy and Zomato continued to evolve and add new features, further cementing their positions as all-in-one solutions for food-related services.

In conclusion, Zeppery faced intense competition from larger, more established food-tech platforms that had already captured significant market share. The dominance of Swiggy and Zomato, combined with their broad range of services and extensive restaurant networks, made it difficult for Zeppery to compete effectively. The competitive pressures, both in terms of user acquisition and restaurant partnerships, significantly contributed to Zeppery's inability to scale and succeed in the market.

7. Customer Experience and App Usability

A key factor in the success of any tech platform, especially in the crowded food-tech market, is the user experience. Zeppery's app, while functional, failed to provide the seamless, intuitive experience that users had come to expect from food-tech platforms. Minor technical issues, a less polished user interface, and slow load times were some of the challenges that early users encountered, contributing to a less-than-ideal experience. This had a direct impact on Zeppery's ability to retain users and drive long-term engagement.

From a usability perspective, Zeppery's app had a simple interface that allowed users to browse restaurants, make reservations, and pre-order meals. However, compared to more established platforms like Swiggy and Zomato, Zeppery's design felt basic and lacked the features that users were accustomed to. For instance, features like personalized recommendations, user reviews, and detailed restaurant profiles, which were standard on competing platforms, were either absent or underdeveloped on Zeppery. This lack of advanced features made the app feel limited in comparison.

One of the major complaints from users was the slow performance of the app, particularly during peak dining hours when users were most likely to be making reservations. The app often experienced lag or took too long to load restaurant menus, which frustrated users who were looking for a quick and efficient way to reserve tables or pre-order food. In the fast-paced world of food-tech, where convenience and speed are paramount, these technical glitches diminished Zeppery's appeal.

Another issue that negatively affected the user experience was the limited number of restaurants available on the platform. Even if the app worked smoothly, users found that there were few dining options to choose from, especially in smaller cities. For those living in Zeppery's core markets, the platform did not provide enough variety to keep them engaged, and as a result, users were more likely to abandon the app after a few uses. The lack of restaurant diversity further hurt Zeppery's ability to retain customers, as many saw little reason to continue using the platform when it failed to meet their dining needs.

Zeppery also struggled to address customer feedback in a timely manner. While early users provided suggestions for improving the app's features and performance, Zeppery's team was slow to roll out updates or address technical issues. This lack of responsiveness frustrated users and gave the impression that Zeppery was not as committed to improving the user experience as its competitors. In contrast, platforms like Swiggy and Zomato regularly updated their apps, adding new features and fixing bugs to enhance the overall experience for users.

Lastly, Zeppery's failure to invest in a strong customer support system further weakened its relationship with users. While competing platforms offered live chat support, easy cancellation processes, and quick refunds, Zeppery's customer support was less robust. Users who encountered issues with reservations or pre-orders often struggled to get timely assistance, leading to negative experiences that deterred them from using the app again. In a market where customer service can make or break user loyalty, Zeppery's shortcomings in this area were a significant drawback.

In conclusion, Zeppery's customer experience and app usability issues played a significant role in its failure to gain widespread adoption. The app's technical glitches, limited features, and lack of responsiveness to customer feedback all contributed to a subpar experience that failed to meet the expectations of modern food-tech users. Without a strong focus on improving usability and addressing user concerns, Zeppery was unable to build the kind of loyal customer base needed to sustain its growth.

8. Funding and Financial Struggles

Like many startups, Zeppery faced significant financial challenges as it attempted to scale. While the initial concept attracted some early investment, Zeppery struggled to secure the level of funding needed to compete with the larger players in the food tech space. Limited financial resources hindered the platform's ability to invest in critical areas such as marketing, technology development, and expanding restaurant partnerships. These financial struggles ultimately played a major role in Zeppery's inability to achieve sustained growth and market penetration.

Zeppery's funding issues stemmed from its inability to prove the scalability of its business model. While investors were excited about the potential for food-tech platforms to disrupt the dining industry, Zeppery's niche offering—focused on pre-ordering meals and streamlining restaurant reservations—did not demonstrate the same high-volume, repeat usage that food delivery platforms were able to show. Investors were wary of pouring significant capital into a platform that, despite its innovative concept, had yet to show strong signs of user adoption and scalability.

One of the key problems was that Zeppery's revenue model relied heavily on commissions from restaurants, but with limited partnerships, the platform's earnings were minimal. Unlike food delivery platforms, which generated revenue from both users and restaurants through delivery fees, Zeppery's revenue streams were more restricted. This meant that even if Zeppery managed to secure more users, its financial viability was tied to forming partnerships with a broader range of restaurants, something it struggled to do. Investors were concerned about the long-term sustainability of this model, especially in an industry where deep-pocketed competitors dominated.

As Zeppery's financial situation worsened, the company found itself in a difficult position. Without adequate funding, Zeppery was unable to invest in marketing campaigns that could have helped drive user growth. This created a vicious cycle where low user adoption led to limited revenue, and limited revenue restricted the company's ability to invest in growth strategies. Meanwhile, competitors like Swiggy and Zomato, backed by substantial venture capital, were able to outspend Zeppery on marketing, promotions, and user acquisition efforts, further widening the gap between Zeppery and the market leaders.

Zeppery's financial struggles also limited its ability to invest in improving its technology. While the app was functional, it lacked the advanced features and user experience improvements that could have helped retain users. Competing platforms were constantly innovating and improving their services, offering users more personalized experiences and faster, more reliable service. Zeppery, on the other hand, was forced to operate with limited resources, resulting in slow updates and an inability to fix technical issues quickly. This, in turn, affected user retention and made it even harder for the platform to grow.

In an effort to raise additional funding, Zeppery's leadership team explored potential pivots to its business model. They considered expanding the platform's offerings to include food delivery or exclusive discounts in an attempt to attract more users. However, these efforts were not enough to convince investors of the platform's long-term viability. With competition in the food tech space intensifying and Zeppery struggling to differentiate itself, investors were hesitant to commit further capital to a platform that had yet to prove its market fit.

In conclusion, Zeppery's funding and financial struggles were a major factor in its inability to scale and compete effectively. The platform's limited revenue streams, combined with its struggles to secure additional investment, made it difficult for Zeppery to invest in the marketing, technology, and partnerships needed for growth. As a result, Zeppery was unable to keep up with its well-funded competitors, ultimately leading to its decline.

9. Attempts to Pivot and Revive the Platform

As Zeppery faced mounting challenges, including low user adoption and limited financial resources, the company made several attempts to pivot and revive the platform. The leadership team recognized that the original concept of pre-ordering food and making restaurant reservations, while innovative, was not enough to compete with the dominant players in the food-tech space. In response, Zeppery explored various strategies to adapt its business model and attract a broader user base, but these efforts ultimately fell short.

One of the first pivots Zeppery attempted was expanding its service offerings to include food delivery. The food delivery market in India was booming, with platforms like Swiggy and Zomato leading the charge. Zeppery hoped that by introducing a delivery option, it could attract more users who were looking for convenience and compete more directly with the major players. However, this pivot came with its own set of challenges. Zeppery lacked the logistical infrastructure needed to handle delivery operations at scale, and without significant investment, it was unable to build a robust delivery network. As a result, the delivery service failed to gain traction.

In addition to exploring food delivery, Zeppery also attempted to introduce exclusive deals and discounts for users who ordered through the app. The idea was to incentivize both customers and restaurants to use the platform by offering discounts that were not available elsewhere. While this strategy initially attracted some attention, it was not enough to sustain long-term growth. Competing platforms like Swiggy and Zomato were already offering similar deals, and with their larger restaurant networks and user bases, they were able to offer more compelling promotions than Zeppery could.

Zeppery also tried to position itself as a premium service, focusing on higher-end restaurants and offering a more curated dining experience. The goal was to differentiate the platform from the mass-market appeal of Swiggy and Zomato by targeting a more affluent customer base that valued quality over convenience. However, this strategy had its own limitations. The premium dining segment was relatively small compared to the broader market, and Zeppery's lack of well-known restaurant partnerships made it difficult to attract high-end users. The platform's limited reach and brand recognition also hindered its ability to succeed in this niche.

Another attempt to pivot involved expanding into new cities and regions. Zeppery hoped that by entering smaller, less competitive markets, it could capture a new audience that was not yet served by the larger food-tech platforms. However, this expansion was hampered by the same issues that plagued Zeppery from the beginning: limited restaurant partnerships and low user adoption. In smaller cities, where consumers were less familiar with tech-driven dining solutions, Zeppery struggled to convince both restaurants and customers of the platform's value.

Despite these efforts, Zeppery was unable to revive the platform or generate significant user growth. The company's pivots, while well-intentioned, were reactive rather than proactive, and they failed to address the underlying issues that had hindered Zeppery's success from the beginning. The platform's lack of differentiation, combined with its struggles to secure funding and partnerships, made it difficult for Zeppery to compete in a market that was increasingly dominated by a few major players.

In conclusion, Zeppery's attempts to pivot and revive the platform were ultimately unsuccessful. While the company explored various strategies, including food delivery, exclusive deals, and premium services, these efforts failed to generate the user growth and market penetration needed to sustain the platform. Zeppery's inability to adapt quickly enough to the competitive landscape, coupled with its limited resources, meant that the platform was unable to recover from its initial struggles.

10. Lessons Learned from Zeppery's Journey

The story of Zeppery provides valuable lessons for startups in the food-tech space and beyond. One of the key takeaways is the importance of forming strong partnerships early on. Zeppery's inability to secure enough restaurant partnerships severely limited its ability to offer users a diverse range of dining options, which in turn hurt its user acquisition efforts. For platforms that rely on partnerships to deliver value, building and maintaining strong relationships with key stakeholders is crucial for success.

Another important lesson from Zeppery's journey is the need for a scalable business model. While Zeppery's pre-ordering concept was innovative, it did not resonate with a large enough audience to sustain growth. Startups need to ensure that their business model can scale and that there is sufficient demand for their product or service. In Zeppery's case, the niche focus on pre-ordering and dine-in experiences limited its appeal in a market where consumers were increasingly gravitating toward food delivery and other conveniences.

Zeppery's struggles also highlight the importance of user experience in the tech industry. The platform's technical glitches, slow performance, and limited features all contributed to low user retention. In a competitive market where consumers have multiple options, offering a seamless and enjoyable user experience is essential. Startups must prioritize investing in their technology and responding to user feedback to ensure that their platform meets the needs of their audience.

Finally, Zeppery's journey underscores the importance of adaptability and innovation in a fast-changing market. While Zeppery made several attempts to pivot and revive the platform, these efforts came too late and failed to address the core issues that had hindered its success. Startups must be willing to adapt quickly to market trends and consumer demands, and they need to be proactive in identifying opportunities for growth rather than reacting to challenges after they arise.

In conclusion, Zeppery's rise and fall offer important lessons about the challenges of scaling a startup in the highly competitive food-tech space. From the need for strong partnerships to the importance of user experience and adaptability, Zeppery's journey serves as a reminder of the many factors that contribute to the success—or failure—of a startup.

Key Points

- **Zeppery's business model** focused on pre-ordering meals and making restaurant reservations, but it struggled to differentiate itself in a competitive food-tech market dominated by delivery-focused platforms like Swiggy and Zomato.
- **Limited partnerships** with restaurants hindered Zeppery's ability to offer a wide variety of choices, which affected user adoption and made it difficult to scale the platform.

- **Low user adoption** was a major issue, as Zeppery failed to attract a critical mass of users due to its narrow focus and lack of compelling incentives compared to established food delivery platforms.
- **Technical and operational challenges** related to app usability, customer service, and real-time coordination with restaurants further weakened Zeppery's ability to deliver a seamless user experience.
- **Zeppery's failure** highlights the importance of strong partnerships, market differentiation, and a robust user experience in succeeding within the competitive food-tech space.

www.ingramcontent.com/pod-product-compliance
Lightning Source LLC
LaVergne TN
LVHW091306150826
845673LV00006B/1561

* 9 7 9 8 8 9 6 1 0 2 0 2 1 *